RECESSION-PROOF CAREER STRATEGIES AFTER COVID

JASON SCHENKER

Copyright © 2020 Prestige Professional Publishing, LLC.

All rights reserved.

RECESSION-PROOF CAREER STRATEGIES AFTER COVID

BY JASON SCHENKER

No part of this publication may be reproduced, copied, stored in or transmitted into a data retrieval system, or transmitted in any form, or by any means (electronic, mechanical, photocopying, recording, or any other method) without written permission of the publisher, Prestige Professional Publishing, LLC.

ISBN: 978-1-946197-60-3 *Paperback*
978-1-946197-57-3 *Ebook*

To everyone struggling in recession.

CONTENTS

PREFACE   7

INTRODUCTION   11

CHAPTER 1
RECESSIONS 101   17

CHAPTER 2
WHAT DOES YOUR PERSONAL RECESSION LOOK LIKE?   33

CHAPTER 3
YOU HAVE OPTIONS   71

CHAPTER 4
PREPARE   83

CHAPTER 5
DIG IN   103

CHAPTER 6
HIDE   117

CHAPTER 7
RUN   137

CHAPTER 8
BUILD   161

CHAPTER 9
INVEST   197

CONTENTS

CHAPTER 10
   NOW WHAT?   **217**

CONCLUSION   **223**

ENDNOTES   **225**

ABOUT THE AUTHOR   **227**
ABOUT PRESTIGE ECONOMICS   **231**
ABOUT THE FUTURIST INSTITUTE   **235**
ABOUT THE PUBLISHER   **237**
DISCLAIMERS   **245**

PREFACE

BEING RECESSION-PROOF

As a global manufacturing recession and a U.S. business investment recession raged during 2015, I wrote the book *Recession-Proof: How to Survive and Thrive in an Economic Downturn* in February 2016. At the time, businesses were under pressure. Fortunately, the recession did not spill over to consumers and the overall U.S. and global economy — despite high risks.

But now things are different. We are in a deep recession.

Businesses and consumers are at risk. And we are in a global recession along the magnitudes of the Great Recession from 2007 to 2009 — if not bigger. Economic recovery after the current pandemic will take time, and the best thing individuals and businesses can do is be prepared and responsive.

In *Recession-Proof Career Strategies After COVID*, I lay out strategic plans for individuals to achieve success even in the face of a downturn. In fact, that is the big idea of this book: to help individuals be recession-proof.

Making Tough Decisions
This book draws on research from Prestige Economics and it represents my attempt to help individuals strategically approach the difficult issue of recession brought on by the COVID-19 pandemic.

Of course, some strategies in this book are easier to implement than others. And I have tried to write this book in a way that starts with some of the most critical basics and then goes on to more complicated strategies, ending with some of the most difficult.

Acknowledgements
No book is done completely alone. There are editorial, design, file conversion, and project management parts of the effort to get a book like this completed. And those tasks require a team.

In many ways, *Recession-Proof: How to Survive and Thrive in an Economic Downturn* was the first edition of this book. And I am grateful to the team that managed the production of that book at Lioncrest. But I am most pleased to have had my own teams at Prestige Economics and Prestige Professional Publishing manage the publication of this book. I am very thankful that they helped make this book a reality.

Along those lines, I want to especially thank **Nawfal Patel**, who managed the production of *Recession-Proof Career Strategies After COVID*. He did a tremendous job managing the team — and my own workflow. I also want to thank **Kerry Ellis** for her fine work creating a new cover of this new book.

Most importantly, I want to thank my family for supporting me in my education, career, entrepreneurship, and authorship.

I am always most grateful for the support of my loving wife, **Ashley Schenker**, and to my wonderful parents, **Janet and Jeffrey Schenker**.

My family supports me in countless ways by providing emotional support and editorial feedback. Every time I write a book, it's a crazy experience that spills over into my family life, so to them and to everyone else who helped me in this process: Thank you!

Finally, thank you for buying this book. I hope *Recession-Proof Career Strategies After COVID* helps you in these uncertain times!

~ Jason Schenker

INTRODUCTION

WHY I WROTE THIS BOOK

In 2001, I finished graduate school and walked right into a recession. I wasn't an economist at the time, but my career was hurt by the economy.

I remember thinking that if I had known a recession was coming, I would have done things differently. My major, graduation timing, and summer job choices would have reflected my knowledge of a coming recession. Unfortunately, they did not.

But because of the 2001 recession, I vowed to become an economist, so I would be able to see the next recession coming — so that the next time, I could be recession-proof.

Not many people get burned by a recession and become an economist to better manage it the next time around, but that's exactly what I did. By the time of the Great Recession of 2007-2009, I was an economist — and this time, I was prepared for it. I used my economic knowhow to run, build, and invest my way out.

One of the things I did was to start my own company, Prestige Economics, and I took it from nothing to where we are now — the world's leading independent commodity and financial market research firm.

Now, with the threat of another U.S. recession on the horizon, I wanted to share what I learned in the last two recessions. I'm sure you've heard the phrase, "If I only knew then, what I know now."

For me, this book contains everything I wish I knew going into the recession of 2001 and the Great Recession. And it includes advice that will help you get through the current recession.

My advice in this book should help you be recession-proof, by showing you how to:

• Predict the next recession with just a few clicks of your mouse
• Turn the bust years into a moneymaking opportunity
• Escape a doomed industry before it's too late
• Keep your job long after your colleagues have been laid off
• Take refuge in a safe-haven sector
• Move where the money is
• Safeguard your retirement
• Survive a charging bull (really)

The next recession is here, and this book should help you be recession-proof, without becoming an economist.

YOU ARE IN GOOD COMPANY

As the Founder, President, and Chief Economist of Prestige Economics, I advise big publicly-traded corporations, small privately-owned companies, and everything in between. Central banks, government bodies, high-net-worth individuals, airlines, oil and gas companies, material handling companies, auto manufacturers, mining companies, transport companies — all of them pay for my advice.

My clients come to me for knowledge about risk management, strategy, economics, and forecasting.

Basically, I help my clients understand their risks — and I help them find upside opportunities in those risks. This is exactly what this book should do for you. This book should help you find upside in an economic downturn.

Aside from helping my clients find upside in their downside risks, they also come to me, because my financial market forecasts and predictions are right, again and again. In fact, I'm one of the most accurate economic forecasters in the world.

Bloomberg News publishes rankings of the most accurate forecasters at predicting what oil, natural gas, metals, currencies, unemployment rates, and so forth are going to do.

Either the price of oil goes over $50 a barrel when you said it would, or it doesn't. This is total accountability, total objectivity — you're putting your money where your mouth is.

So when I tell you that Prestige Economics has been top ranked for forecasts across almost every quarter that we've been forecasting, and that we've been top-ranked in 43 different categories, you can be sure that it's not just hype. And you can be sure that my advice can help you in recession — and recovery.

FOREWARNED IS FOREARMED

I wrote this book to give you the upper hand that I give to my clients. When people hear the name of my company, they often think that the word "prestige" refers to my company's solid gold reputation.

But that's not actually how I intended it. *Prestige* is derived from a French word meaning "trick" — think of the movie *The Prestige*, which is about magicians and their secrets. Prestige Economics is all about pulling the curtain away from the wizard, seeing how the rabbit emerges from the hat. It's about demystifying this mysterious thing, the global economy, seeing its tricks and sleight-of-hand, and arming clients with tricks of their own to get the best of it.

That's what my services provide, and that's what I'm offering you in this book. So don't give in to the fear. You'll make it through with sound knowledge and smart decisions. You'll make the right gambles, and you'll have the best backup plans in place if they don't work out.

With this book, you'll be ready to survive and thrive in the current recession, whatever that recession looks like for you.

Although the advice in this book is designed to be helpful after the COVID-19 pandemic, it is my hope that the strategies in this book will be able to help those who go through future, subsequent economic downturns.

There's a reason why people call the dynamics of the economy a business cycle. It's because there are repeating patterns of growth and recession. And in the future you may again face challenges.

But being forewarned is being forearmed. And even in recession, there is the opportunity to survive and thrive — there is the chance to find upside in a downturn.

With all that in mind, let's get started!

After all, when it comes to being recession-proof — there's no time like the present.

CHAPTER 1

RECESSIONS 101

Before we go too deeply into our discussion of recession, I should explain what a recession is. Economists say that the country has gone into a recession if there have been *two consecutive quarterly declines in growth, as reflected by Gross Domestic Product.* That's just a fancy way of saying that the country has been producing less and less stuff for six months. And a more recent definition from the National Bureau of Economic Research is even simpler, and it shows that the United States is in a recession right now.

A recession is when business activity and income fall across the nation. It's when companies are getting smaller, workers are losing their jobs, families are tightening their belts, and everyone is stressing out. The rhythmic up and down in the economy has a name: the business cycle. The "up" parts are called growth or expansion. They are heady times when everyone seems to be getting jobs, raises, and fat bonuses. People are growing their businesses, making money on the stock market, buying cars, and feeling lucky. The "down" parts are the recession, when everyone is freaking out and cutting back.

The up part of the business cycle sets up the conditions for the down part, and the down part sets up the conditions for the up part.

It's almost a natural law, like the swaying of a pendulum, and it's been happening for centuries.

Economists usually explain it like this: when the economy is growing, everyone has more money in their pockets, so businesses can charge more for things. Now everything costs more, so each dollar is worth a little less than it used to be. This is called *inflation*. You don't want too much inflation, because then people lose confidence in the value of money, and all hell breaks loose. The genie gets out of the bottle and it's very hard to put it back in.

There's an old story from Germany after World War I. It was a time of hyperinflation, when inflation was out of control and cash was getting less and less valuable by the *hour*. A man brought a wheelbarrow full of German Marks to a store to buy a loaf of bread. He went into the store and when he came back out, someone had stolen the wheelbarrow, but left the money.

That's the situation you *don't* want.

To stave off inflation, the central bank (in the United States, it's called the Federal Reserve) raises the interest rate (the "price of money") to make it more expensive for people to get loans.

Now there's less money around, so businesses can't keep growing and raising prices. Economic growth slows, which slows inflation. Sadly, business contracts. Families cut their expenses.

Et voilà, recession.

Eventually the central bank feels satisfied that it has put the inflation genie back into the bottle. So it lowers the interest rate, making it easy again to get money to invest in things. As people and companies access this money and invest it, growth picks up, and the cycle starts all over again. Central banks have a really tough row to hoe in balancing the need to fight inflation and with the need to encourage growth.

The difference between recession and inflation is like the difference between losing your job and having your house burn down. Recessions can have really negative, immediate impacts on people's lives. But too much inflation can destroy the wealth of an entire country.

An even easier way to understand the business cycle is to think about the *feelings* that people are experiencing.

In an economic upswing, everyone is feeling optimistic and cocky and happily spending lots of money. They're so exuberant that they *over*spend, and buy things they don't need, or invest in stupid things that aren't going to pay off. Eventually they realize how much they've overspent and they get scared. Then it's slash and burn time! They pull the plug on their new business ventures and hunker down.

Once the marching order is to cut, cut, cut, it's all over. The more they do this, the more they're creating the very downturn that they're afraid of. That's a recession.

And if it gets bad enough, it can become a depression.

It's like that famous line in *Dirty Harry*: "Are you feeling lucky, punk?" When people are feeling lucky, there's growth. When people aren't feeling lucky, there's contraction — and recession.

This means that a recession is partly a self-fulfilling prophecy. It happens partly because we think it's going to happen. But that doesn't make it any less real, or any less inevitable. Remember the scene in the movie *The Matrix* where Neo meets the Oracle. The Oracle tells Neo, "Don't worry about the vase." Just then he turns and knocks it over, shattering it. Neo apologizes, and the Oracle says, "I said don't worry about it... What's really going to bake your noodle later on is, would you still have broken it if I hadn't said anything?"

THE BUSINESS CYCLE IN THREE WORDS OR LESS

Actually, there is an even simpler way of explaining the business cycle. Let me get to it by way of a story. In early 2004, I was hired by Wachovia as an economist. Wachovia is now a part of Wells Fargo Bank, but at the time, Wachovia was an absolutely massive bank in its own right — the third or fourth largest bank in the United States, depending on how you measured it — and I was tasked with keeping an eye on things like inflation, the automobile industry, and a bunch of other important bellwethers of where the global economy was heading.

I'd been at the job for just a month, and I noticed something. Inflation was going up. Oil prices were going up. I was fresh out of my Master's degree in Applied Economics, so I used some of the fancy statistics I had been taught, plugged in these numbers, and I made a prediction that caught a lot of people by surprise. My prediction was this: oil prices would go over $50 a barrel before the end of the year.

Nobody believed me at first. Oil prices were in the $30s at the time, and going above $50 seemed crazy. I remember when a reporter at NBC Nightly News called me up just to laugh at me and my silly prediction.

At the end of September of that year, I was in Houston, and it happened. Oil had been rising for months. It finally hit $50 for the first time — and it kept climbing. I had been right.

That prediction earned me a new job title, practically overnight. I was now the Chief Energy Economist for Wachovia, this enormous bank, after having worked there for just a little over six months. But I haven't even gotten to the important point of the story yet.

The point of the story comes *after* getting my new job title. My desk was on the same floor as the foreign exchange traders, so I always saw them around. One day a couple of these guys came over to my desk and started talking to me. They said, "Jason, we saw your forecast for the price of oil. That was a really good forecast. You're a good economist. You really went out on a limb there, but you were right."

Now, these guys weren't usually so quick to dole out compliments, so at this point I was waiting for the other shoe to drop. I said, "Uh, thanks guys…"

They quickly responded, "Yeah sure. You're good, but we want to know if you're a *great* economist. So we're going to give you a little pop quiz. Just one question."

There I was, new at the company, new at my job, with this high-flying job title, and the CEO of the company had been quoting me here and there. I really didn't want to mess up and answer the question wrong. And I was expecting something really tough.

Then they asked the question: "What two things drive markets?" I remembered thinking, no problem! This question is a softball across the plate! So I said, "That's easy. Supply and demand."

The traders hung their heads in disappointment.

They said, "We thought you were better than that." I said, "What do you mean?

If it's not supply and demand, what is it?"

They said, "The two things that drive markets are *fear* and *greed*."

Fear and greed. It's not a nice way of putting it, but it's basically right. It's an assessment that traders and analysts would call "directionally correct." So let me explain the business cycle one last time — this time in terms of *fear* and *greed*.

It starts with greed. There's a cherry tree that is just sagging from the weight of delicious, ripe cherries. So people get greedy. They pick the cherries right off the tree with their bare hands, in a total frenzy, until all the low-hanging cherries are gone. Then they buy cherry pickers and start picking away at the higher branches. They're doing so well that they splurge and replace their ordinary cherry pickers with gold-plated cherry pickers, because why not? Times are good! Now everyone's picking cherries with these expensive, extravagant cherry pickers, and pretty soon there are no cherries left.

Then the greed becomes fear. Everyone panics, runs away from the tree, sells their cherry pickers, and hides out.

That's a recession.

A year later, the cherries have grown back. Everyone goes back into greed mode, and buys diamond-encrusted, touch-screen-operated cherry pickers with built-in Wi-Fi and massage chair attachments, and just goes nuts on that cherry tree. And repeat.

I watch and report on that cherry tree for a living. The insights in the coming chapters will help you stay ahead of the cherry-picking game.

FEAR AND GREED ECONOMICS

Figure 1-1 illustrates the economics of fear and greed. As you can see, when greed is high and fear is low, investment is high. However, when fear is high and greed is low, investment is low.

RECESSION WATCH

How do you know when a recession is coming? Economists have written many, many millions of pages on this question. But it all boils down to a few simple things:

Warning signs. Unemployment drops significantly. The U.S. Federal Reserve gets nervous that the good times are getting a little *too* good. So it raises interest rates — the price of borrowing money to start or expand a business. This is something that happened most recently in 2018.

That means the good times are getting a little too good, and they've decided to put the brakes on. Hello, recession.

Figure 1-1: Fear and Greed Economics

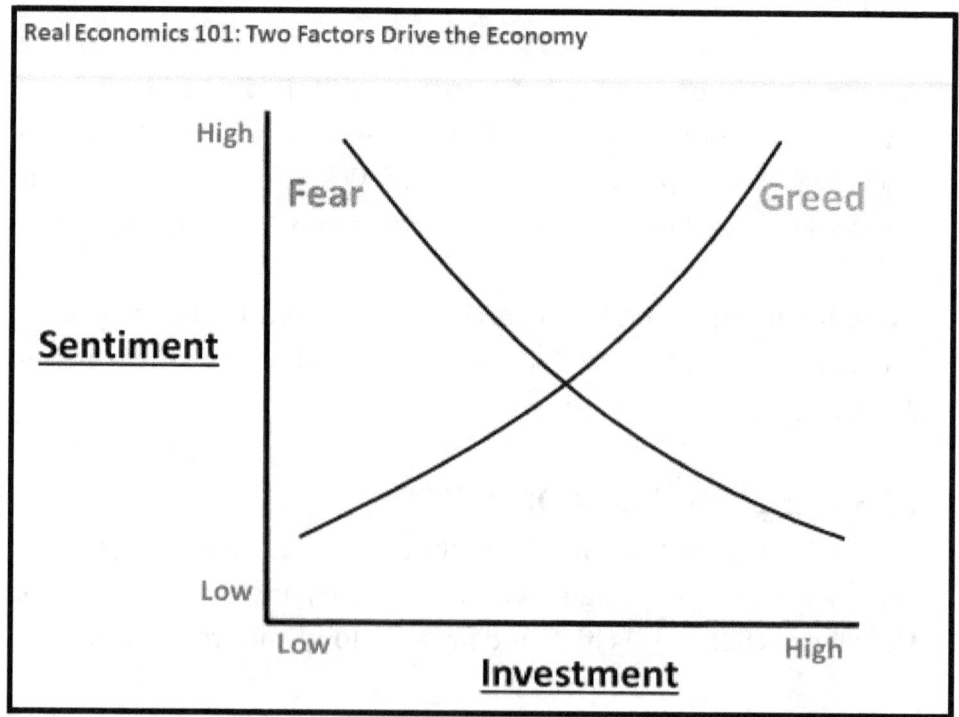

Rising risks. China's economy slows down. China produces goods for the rest of the world, so if it slows, this is a bad sign for the global economy. China also consumes a huge proportion of all the stuff — fuel, food, raw materials — in the world. If it's doing poorly, so is everyone else. This was going on in 2018 and 2019 — and got a lot worse in the first half of 2020.

The danger zone. The U.S. ISM Manufacturing Index falls below 50 — its break-even. That means U.S. manufacturing is contracting and stuff isn't being made. If the same happens to the Eurozone Manufacturing PMI and the Chinese Caixin Manufacturing PMI, that's bad for global manufacturing. In Figure 1-2, you can see that's exactly what was happening in early 2020.

Figure 1-2: Global Manufacturing PMIs[1]

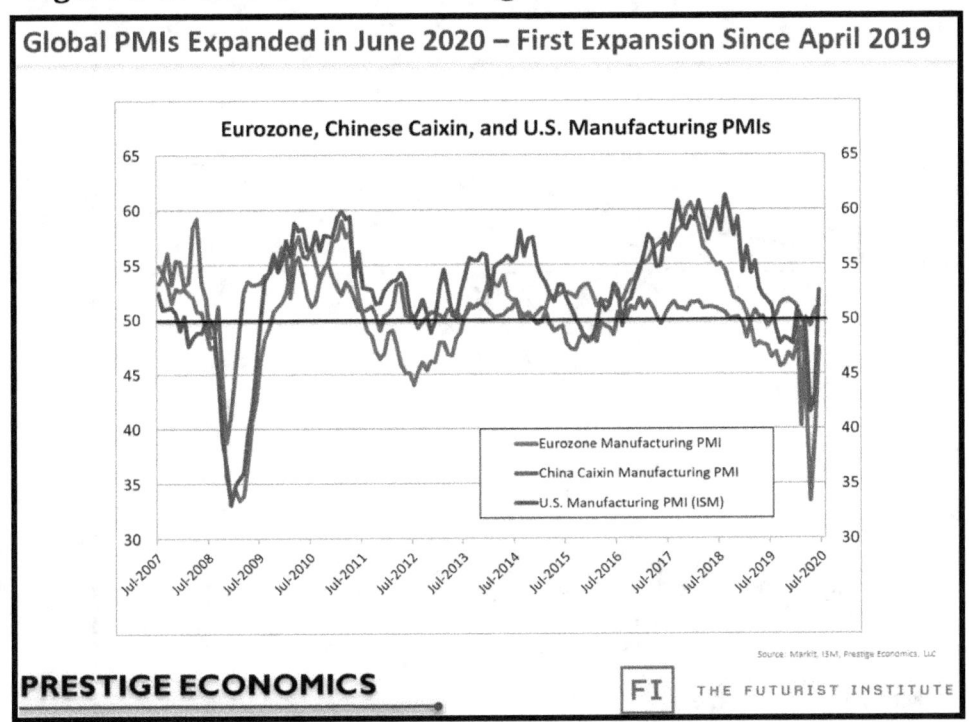

In fact, the global manufacturing and investment slowdown was already in play during 2018 and 2019 — before the COVID-19 pandemic and recession. And the July 2020 IMF forecasts for recovery shown in Figure 1-3 reflect expectations of a gradual recovery in global GDP.

Figure 1-3: IMF Recovery Forecasts[2]

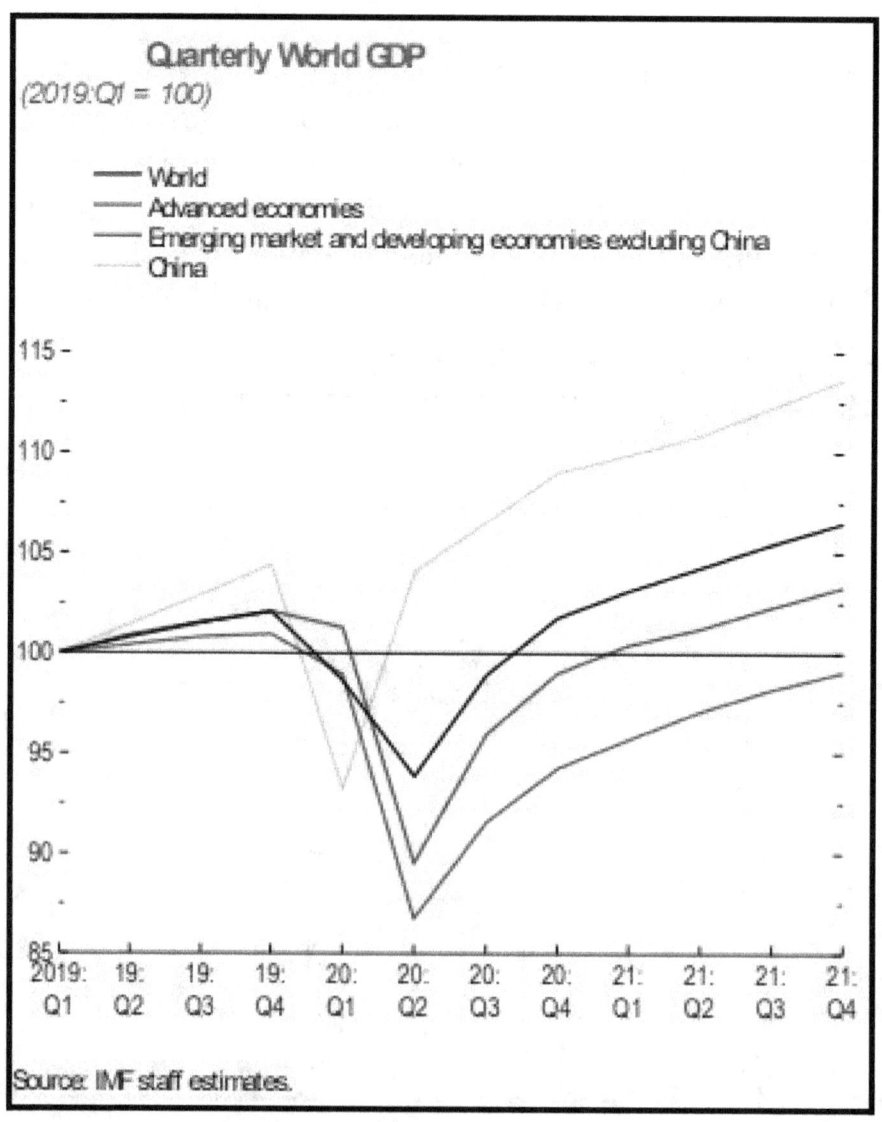

Figure 1-3 also shows that the recovery is likely to be slowest for advanced economies, with the total level of GDP across advanced economies unlikely to reach Q1 2019 levels even by Q4 2021. This means that advanced economies may not reach Q4 2019 pre-recession levels until sometime in mid– or late-2022.

The outlook for emerging and developing economies is stronger than for advanced economies. But there is likely to be a gap of lost growth that persists far into the future. And this is true for advanced as well as emerging market, developing economies.

In April 2020, the outlook for the global economy was quite dire, with the share of countries with IMF forecasts reflecting negative per capita growth in Figure 1-4 likely to exceed the highest levels during the 2007-2009 recession.

Figure 1-4: Magnitude of Recession[3]

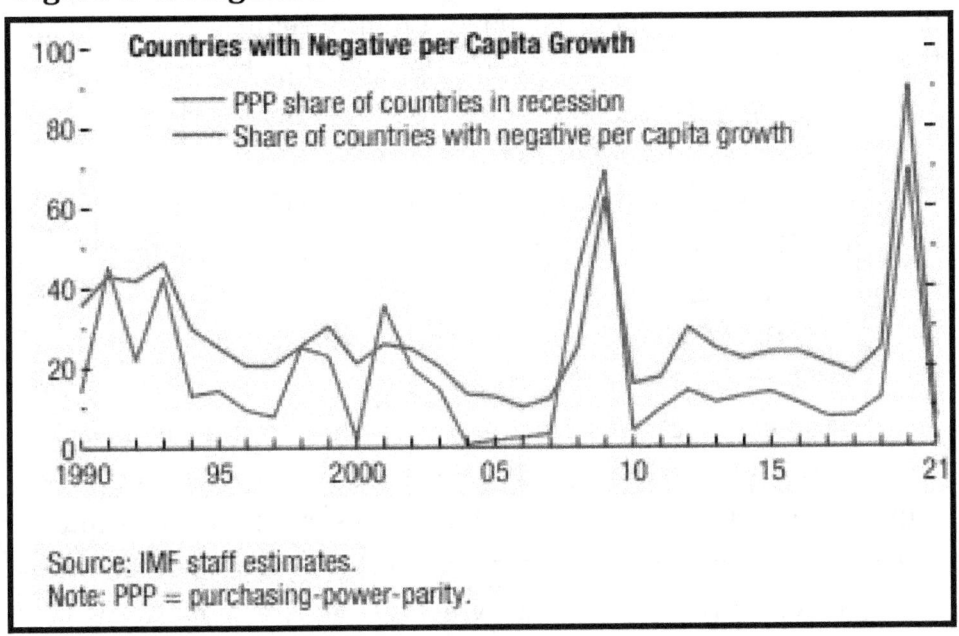

As another critical data point of recession, the share of countries expected by the IMF to experience PPP (purchasing power parity) recessions as of April 2020 was also likely to be comparable to the percentage seen during the Great Recession. This, too, is shown in Figure 1-4.

The IMF forecasts of global and country GDP growth rates shown in Figure 1-5 were published in June 2020 and included predictions of deep worldwide recession. The outlooks for the United States and advanced economies were particularly weak.

THE ORIGINS OF RECESSION: MURDER

In January 2019, equity markets under pressure were met with policy communication and forward-guidance designed to simulate economic growth. The 2019 panel included the current Fed Chairman — Jay Powell — as well as the last two chairs of the Federal Reserve, Janet Yellen and Ben Bernanke. At the time, Bernanke shared a critical quote. He said that business cycles "don't die of old age…they get murdered." And he was right!

— In 2001, the economy was murdered by a tech bubble.
— In 2007-2009, the economy was murdered by a housing bubble and financial crisis.
— In 2020, the COVID-19 pandemic murdered global growth.

That 2019 Fed panel boosted equity markets significantly in early 2019, but COVID-19 still triggered a recession in 2020. And one thing seem certain looking ahead: business cycles will continue. In the future, business cycles at risk of getting murdered will again present threats to GDP growth, jobs, and stock markets.

JOBS IN RECESSION

Of course, one of the most painful parts about a recession is joblessness and unemployment. But it's important to know that equity markets are not GDP, and GDP is not the job market.

As this book went to print in early July 2020, there were some significantly weak jobs data out of the United States. And they told two very different stories.

Figure 1-5: IMF Growth Forecasts — June 2020[4]

Overview of the *World Economic Outlook* Projections
(Percent change, unless noted otherwise)

			Year over Year	
			Projections	
	2018	2019	2020	2021
World Output	3.6	2.9	–4.9	5.4
Advanced Economies	2.2	1.7	–8.0	4.8
United States	2.9	2.3	–8.0	4.5
Euro Area	1.9	1.3	–10.2	6.0
Germany	1.5	0.6	–7.8	5.4
France	1.8	1.5	–12.5	7.3
Italy	0.8	0.3	–12.8	6.3
Spain	2.4	2.0	–12.8	6.3
Japan	0.3	0.7	–5.8	2.4
United Kingdom	1.3	1.4	–10.2	6.3
Canada	2.0	1.7	–8.4	4.9
Other Advanced Economies 3/	2.7	1.7	–4.8	4.2
Emerging Market and Developing Economies	4.5	3.7	–3.0	5.9
Emerging and Developing Asia	6.3	5.5	–0.8	7.4
China	6.7	6.1	1.0	8.2
India 4/	6.1	4.2	–4.5	6.0
ASEAN-5 5/	5.3	4.9	–2.0	6.2
Emerging and Developing Europe	3.2	2.1	–5.8	4.3
Russia	2.5	1.3	–6.6	4.1
Latin America and the Caribbean	1.1	0.1	–9.4	3.7
Brazil	1.3	1.1	–9.1	3.6
Mexico	2.2	–0.3	–10.5	3.3
Middle East and Central Asia	1.8	1.0	–4.7	3.3
Saudi Arabia	2.4	0.3	–6.8	3.1
Sub-Saharan Africa	3.2	3.1	–3.2	3.4
Nigeria	1.9	2.2	–5.4	2.6
South Africa	0.8	0.2	–8.0	3.5

On the one hand, data misspecification errors in the May 2020 U.S. employment report showed an unemployment rate of 13.3 percent. But the weekly jobless claims data pointed to much higher levels of joblessness as well as a likely higher unemployment rate. In fact, jobless claims for the week ending 20 June 2020 were over 19.5 million, which about three times higher than they were at the peak of 6.6 million in the prior recession.

Equity markets rebounded quickly from lows in March 2020. But the labor market is like an escalator on the way down — and an elevator on the way up.

Put simply, joblessness rises much more quickly than it falls.

Figure 1-6: Jobless Claims[5]

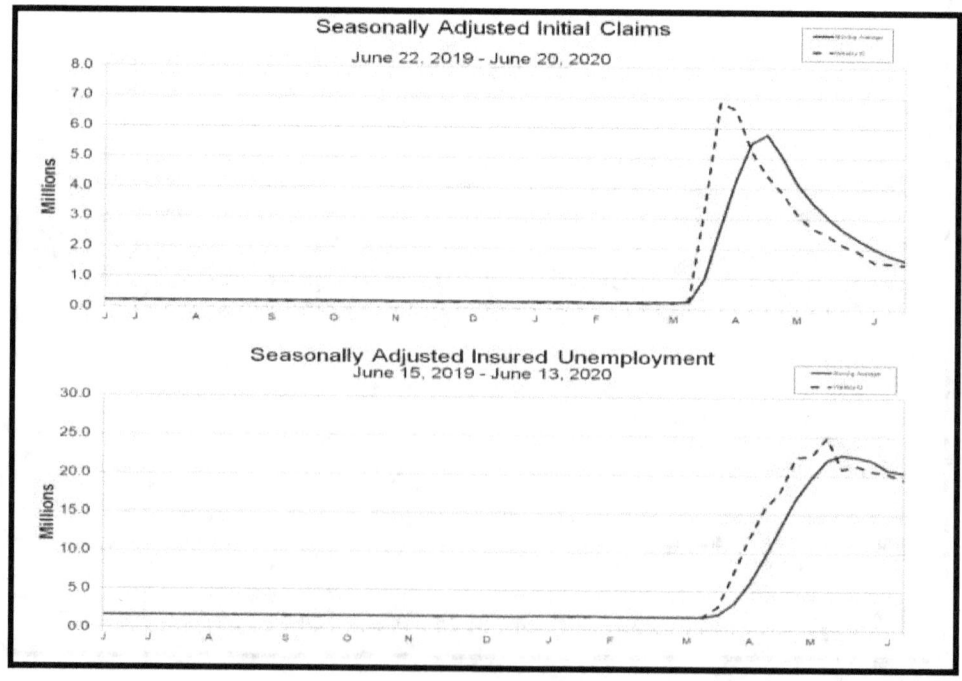

CHAPTER SUMMARY

- Markets are driven by two factors: *fear* and *greed*.

- The traditional definition of a recession is two consecutive quarterly declines in growth, as reflected by GDP.

- The ISM Manufacturing Index is a critical leading indicator of U.S. manufacturing activity and total GDP growth.

- Chinese consumption of global commodities is high, and a weak China hints at weak global manufacturing — and weak global growth.

- U.S. unemployment is an important indicator of the health of the U.S. job market, and a critical factor for setting Fed policy. Recent jobless claims data show that over 47 million Americans lost their jobs in a 14-week period and almost 20 million Americans are unemployed.

CHAPTER 2

WHAT DOES YOUR PERSONAL RECESSION LOOK LIKE?

THE TWO DUMBEST THOUGHTS I EVER HAD

I'm here to offer you some wisdom. But first, let me share some foolishness with you. I'm going to tell you about the two dumbest thoughts I ever had.

The second dumbest thought I ever had.

It was a sunny spring day in 1999, and I had just gotten out of an economics class at the University of Virginia. There I was, standing in the sunshine on The Lawn of this beautiful historic Grounds, and everything seemed right in the universe. I was finishing up my undergrad, and I had an offer to pursue a Master's in German at the University of North Carolina, Chapel Hill.

It was a full ride — tuition, health insurance, living allowance, everything. It was tremendous funding for a graduate student.

On top of that, all of my friends in similar degree programs were landing six-figure consulting jobs right out of college. It was the era of the supercharged dot-com boom — the best job market in the history of the United States. I knew I could easily score a good job in the private sector if I wanted it. I was spoiled with two great options, and I wasn't sure which to go for. I liked being a student, and I wanted to learn more, so I figured that I'd go for the grad school option.

After all, *if the economy is rocking now, just think how great it will be in a few more years! And by then I'll have a Master's degree, so I'll make even* more *money!*

That was the second dumbest thought I ever had. I wasn't thinking like an economist. I wasn't thinking about the business cycle, the inevitability of bad times following good. I wasn't thinking about the way that the economy can kick you in the ass. Of course, I wasn't yet an economist. So I signed up for grad school, I got my Master's, and I re-entered the job market in the spring of 2001.

Oh, what a difference two years makes!

The same companies that were offering $10,000, $15,000, or $25,000 signing bonuses in the fall of 2000 were now shedding employees like they were going out of style. I met people who had received written job offers in 1999 or 2000, and then the companies deferred them for a year or two. A number of those deferrals became permanent, as many people never, ever received those jobs.

If it's good now, it'll be even better tomorrow! That's the second dumbest thought I ever had. It's a lesson I learned before I became a business economist, and it's the most important thing about the economy that I share with people who are not economists.

The #1 dumbest thought I ever had.

This thought was even worse than the last one. *This* thought didn't just mess up my career. It nearly got me killed. July 12th, 1997. Pamplona, Spain. I'm 20 years old and I'm at the festival of San Fermín, with its world-famous Running of the Bulls. I'm a dude, I'm just out of my teenage years, so I make like Hemingway and decide to participate in the run, risks be damned.

You may have seen videos of guys dressed in red and white running through this incredibly tiny, narrow lane on the way to the bullfighting arena, nearly getting trampled and gored by the dozens of bulls that are running right next to them. What those videos don't tell you—and what *I* didn't know either—is that it doesn't end there.

No, it doesn't end there. I make it to the arena in one piece, and some guys pen up the bulls. But then they let the "baby bulls" out to play. These bulls are just one or two years old, and they have tapered horns so they can't gore you. But even so, they're a good 350 to 500 pounds each.

So "playing" is sort of a misleading word.

This isn't the running of the bulls. This is the *real* action. This is the thing no one warned you about. This is the unknown unknown.

I'm thinking, "I like the action. Let's see how this goes."

It's 7:00 in the morning, the arena is packed with spectators, and there's a five-and-a-half-foot-high white wall separating the spectators from the big baby bruisers in the arena. That wall keeps the spectators safe, and it keeps the guys in the arena, like me, not so safe.

The first thing I see is a baby bull chasing a guy while he's trying to run away. Despite what you might think, that doesn't work. The baby bull catches up to the guy and butts him into the air like a soccer ball, once, then twice.

Then the baby bull runs over him, twice for good measure. The guy is not looking happy at this point. Two medics climb into the arena, put the beat-up guy on a stretcher, and take him to safety. The second thing I see is a baby bull running towards another guy, and the guy puts his hands up in front of his face. Despite conventional wisdom, this does not make the bull go away. The bull tramples him, then turns around and tramples him again.

Apparently, bulls like doing things in twos.

The medics come back — they are definitely kept busy this morning — and carry this second victim to safety. I'm still standing there in the arena.

The third thing that I see is another baby bull getting frisky. Luckily there are a good 25 or 30 guys between me and this baby bull. I'm totally safe, right?

Not quite. The bull veers left and the bull veers right; people are running out of the way, and suddenly, all the people are gone and the bull is coming straight for me. The first guy taught me that I can't run. The second guy taught me that I can't hide.

So, the question now is, what *can* I do?

I remembered an old cliché: *grab the bull by the horns*.

It's all I can think of, so it's what I do.

The bull comes at me, hits my stomach hard with his nose, and I grab his horns from underneath. This sounds like an awesome strategy, but there's an unknown unknown here, too. What they don't tell you is that when you are holding a bull by his horns, and his face is in your stomach, you don't see where you're going and neither does the bull. Well, I keep holding on, leaning forward onto his neck to steady myself, and the bull is running, veering, jostling, with no idea where he's going, and I have no idea either, and all I know is that I'm now riding a bull and he's drooling copiously down my leg.

Finally we land in the dirt. Since I had leaned forward onto his neck, I actually slide pretty gently onto the ground, and I'm okay. I've got drool-encrusted sand all over my pant leg, but I'm otherwise unscathed.

You can't run, you can't hide, but if you grab the bull by the horns, you're going to make it. It might not be pretty, it might not be fun, and you'll probably get a little drool on you, but everybody can survive a little drool. Believe it or not, I haven't gotten to the climax of this story, or *The Dumbest Thought I Ever Had*.

Now they take the baby bulls away, and it's time to double down. I'm still in the arena. Apparently I still like the action. I hear an announcement over the loudspeakers, and immediately everyone in the arena starts jumping over the walls, trying to get to safety. It looks like Looney Tunes with people's legs kicking in the air.

The announcement is in Basque, not Spanish, so I haven't understood a word of it. I'm standing there, about 40 feet from the wall and maybe 60 feet from the center of the arena, totally blindsided, wondering what's going on.

I don't wonder for long. Just then, a big bull enters the arena, near where I am. I'm talking about a giant, full-grown, 2,000-pound monster bull that some matador is going to fight that night. His horns sparkle in the morning sun. I'm not kidding.

They *sparkle* — and they are *not* tapered. It's like a Greek tragedy — trial after trial after trial. You do the running and you think you're done. You survive the baby bulls and you think you're done. Then the big bulls get in on the action.

The full-grown bull stomps to the middle of the arena, facing away from me.

So here's the dumbest thought I ever had: *that bull ain't gonna turn around.*

Of course he does turn around. He faces me, puts his head down, stomps the ground twice — thump, thump — like something out of a cartoon.

Now I'm thinking, "Maybe this was a little too much action." I start running for the wall.

Spectators are waving me forward. I remember a particular woman who was looking at me with an expression of total shock and terror. When I get about halfway to the wall, they stop waving me on. Now their faces go blank and their hands fall to their sides. I can hear the bull's hooves stomping behind me. That is by far the scariest thing I've ever heard.

The assumption is I'm going to be skewered against the wall by this one-ton bull. That bull ain't gonna turn around. Yeah, right.

But here is where I had some luck. I grew up in New England, with its cold winters, so I spent a lot of time in gym class indoors, and I got pretty good at gymnastics. My specialty was pikes. I wasn't so good at the *landings*, but I was good at the jumps. So there I am in the arena, fleeing the bull, and I hit the wall running. It's five and a half feet tall, but I'm six foot three.

I put my two hands up in front of me and I launch straight up in the air, a complete pike. I hear five thousand spectators suck in their breaths all at once.

I go straight up in the air, and I fall headfirst into the concrete stands, using my elbows to break my fall. It's messy. My arms get scratched on the concrete, and I'm bleeding a little. I still have scars on my elbows from that fall.

But I'm okay.

When I get up, that same woman who had the look of horror on her face makes a motion with her hands. She holds them about a foot apart and says, "*Toro, toro.*" She could see how close that bull came to goring me; it must have been just 12 or 18 inches. At this point, I look over the wall into the arena, and the bull is standing right there.

The things you do when you're young.

But the point of this story, and the reason that I open every speech I give with this story, is this: a recession is a 2,000-pound bull of the economy.

Just like in that arena, you've got to grab the bull by the horns.

It won't be pretty, it might be confusing and unpleasant, and you'll probably get spit-encrusted sand all over your pants, but you can make it out in one piece.

What you can't do is just stand there and say, "Hey, let's just see how this full-sized bull thing turns out."

THE BULL ECONOMY

When it comes to surviving and thriving in a recession, there are some thoughts that a lot of people have that are just as dumb as the belief *that bull ain't gonna turn around*. I already shared one of those thoughts:

"If the economy is rocking now, just think how great it will be in a few more years!"

And here are a few others:

"I don't need to build a network outside of the company where I work. There will always be work for me here at ABC Industries."

"I'm an expert in my job. Why should I get more training? No one could ever replace me."

"My company is laying people off left, right, and center, but that's okay. I'm indispensable. I'll just hunker down at my company and wait for the recession to pass."

The sad truth is, people with these kinds of attitudes — and many people have these kinds of attitudes, even if they don't realize it themselves — are probably not going to be okay in the coming economic downturn. In all likelihood, they are going to get gored.

But here's the good news: just by picking up this book, you are ahead of the game. Whether you're reading it when things are still good, or if your personal recession has already started, you have options.

And having options is the name of the game.

Recessions take options away; this book develops and maintains them. You can minimize the damage personally and professionally. You may even use a recession as an opportunity — a chance to get more education, become more valuable for your company, start a business, or buy low into the market. You can even think about your perfect job and how to get there.

RECESSIONS, BIG AND SMALL

Recessions come in lots of shapes and sizes. We often think of them as national and international events. If you watch CNBC or read the *Wall Street Journal*, they talk about these enormous global downturns like the Great Recession or the Great Depression. But a recession can also be much more surgical in how it hits. Let me give you some examples.

A recession can hit a specific *region* or even an individual city.

Detroit took a big hit during the Great Recession. But a less publicized example that I know personally is Fall River, Massachusetts. I grew up just outside of it. Fall River is an old mill town, and it has been in recession for over a *century*. It was rocking back around the time of the Civil War.

At one point, it was the most important textile city in the world.

But then that industry went from New England to the Southeast, from the Southeast to Mexico, from Mexico to China, from China to India and Malaysia, and now to Africa.

The rest of the country goes up and down, but that town doesn't — it's a mill town that hasn't reinvented itself, so it stays in recession. Even when times are good, there are limits to how good things are.

Over the last 25 years, the healthy job market of Austin stands in stark contrast to the lack of jobs in Detroit and Fall River. You can see the unemployment rates of these three markets in Figure 2-1.

Figure 2-1: Regional Unemployment Rates[1]

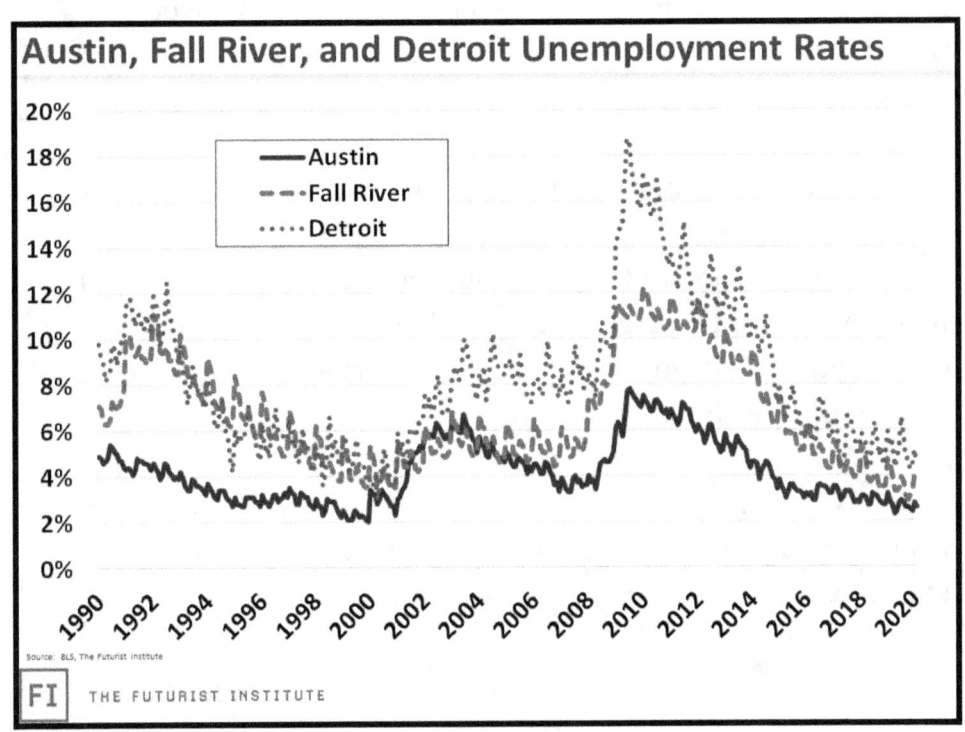

A recession isn't a simple, monolithic thing. In late 2009, just after the Great Recession — when unemployment was at its worst — some parts of the United States were still doing fine.

Now, some of the hardest-hit parts of the country, like the Rust Belt, were showing improvements, but other parts weren't. For example, the Southwest and the Southeast were slower to recover.

A recession can hit workers in a specific *industry*.

For instance, manufacturing has been weakening for decades.

First jobs were exported and outsourced and then people were replaced by machines. If you're a human worker in manufacturing, you've probably been feeling the pinch of all that outsourcing and automation for some time.

If you haven't lost your job already, you're afraid of losing it soon.

Right now, people are talking about the "Internet of everything." In a few years they're going to be talking about the "automation of everything." If you're a tollbooth worker or a cashier, the machines have already come for you.

If you work in a risky industrial environment where wages, insurance, and workers' comp are huge expenses, beware. The machines are coming for your job, too.

A recession can hit a specific *sector*.

In 2000-2001, it was the technology sector.

The dot-com bubble burst, and people in the technology industry were left reeling. In 2007 to 2009, it was housing.

During the industrial and Chinese manufacturing recession between 2014 and 2016, the price of a barrel of oil was cut by more than half in just a year.

Good news for car owners, bad news for the millions of Americans employed in the oil industry. This sector impact can also have a regional impact. For example, Texas and Houston unemployment rates fell faster than the national level coming out of the Great Recession, because oil prices were solid.

Currently, the outlook for Texas and Houston is gloomier than for the total U.S. economy, because the U.S. oil and gas sector is once again in a recession due to mandated significant petroleum fuels demand destruction.

Plus, there are significant risks to tourism and travel. This could adversely impact the economic health of specific tourism-centric regions like Orlando, Las Vegas, Hawaii, and New Orleans.

And there are also risks to service businesses and housing in the current recession. But the extent of the risks remains to be seen.

A recession can hit a specific *company*.

The perfect example of that is Blockbuster Video. You probably know what happened here. Blockbuster's fall was so steady and complete and devastating that it's become a textbook example of what not to do.

Streaming services like Netflix burst on the scene, Blockbuster clung to its old brick-and-mortar, corner-store-video-rental business model, and the results were not pretty. If you were an employee of Blockbuster, it didn't matter to you what the Dow Jones was doing, or what the overall economy looked like. For you, depending completely on that one company, all that mattered was the surgical-strike recession hitting *you*.

Think about it.

Somebody was the last dude to be laid off from Blockbuster.

There was someone there at the end. Don't be that dude. Why do some places and companies and industries do well while others do poorly?

Here's a couple of things to keep in mind. When a recession happens, people have less money. When you have less money, what kinds of things are you going to continue buying? You're definitely going to continue buying food.

The result: farming regions and grocery stores do okay during a recession.

What are you going to stop buying?

You're probably going to think twice about that extravagant family vacation to Disney World. The result: tourism-dependent places like Florida, and industries like leisure and hospitality, are hit hard. People aren't going to choose a trip to the Bahamas over buying groceries any time soon.

Well, they might, but they shouldn't, and they usually don't.

There are fancy words to describe how different industries experience the up and downs of the business cycle.

Most industries and businesses do well when the economy does well, and these are called *procyclical* businesses. Some industries like tourism and leisure are very procyclical, and when the economy is growing, they experience big booms, but when recession hits, these industries suffer big busts.

In contrast to procyclical businesses, some industries actually do *better* during a recession (like musical instruments and junk food), and these are called *counter-cyclical*.

Finally, some industries do okay all the time (like staple foods), and they are called *acyclical*, because the business cycle doesn't affect them.

The important thing here isn't the fancy academic terms, but the idea that recession affects businesses and industries differently.

DRILL #1: FORCES BEYOND YOUR CONTROL

List 10 forces beyond your control that could cause you to lose your job in the next 12 months:

1. _____

2. _____

3. _____

4. _____

5. _____

6. _____

7. _____

8. _____

9. _____

10. _____

A recession isn't one big thing — it's a lot of little things. It's those little things that you, as an individual, experience. A recession can hit a specific *family* or *individual* — like yourself.

You've probably gone through one or two personal recessions during your life. It might come about from a big global recession, a national recession, or any of these more specific recessions I just mentioned: region, city, industry, sector, company.

Wherever it comes from, the emotional experience is similar. You're so worried about losing your job that you can't relax — it's on your mind every day. Your colleagues get laid off and your workload goes up to compensate for it. Now you're doing double or triple the work you did before, while also suffering a pay cut. Plus, there's nothing you can do about it, because if you complain, you'll get the axe.

Your stress levels shoot up. You don't have time to spend with your kids. You worry about your income. You worry about paying your mortgage. You worry about paying for your children's education. You might even worry about putting food on the table.

Then you lose your job, and everything goes from bad to worse. Recessions take a huge personal toll — not just on people's mental health, but on their physical health, too. A recent article by Harvard and Stanford professors found that people who are worried about losing their jobs are 50 percent more likely to report poor health. It also found that working long hours makes you 35 percent more likely to be diagnosed with an illness, and 20 percent more likely to *die* in any given year.

Your personal recession might be as "mild" as cutting back on your vacations and your fine dining, or it might be as devastating as losing your house. However big or small it is, it's scary and it's stressful. You feel like you don't have options. You feel like your world is falling apart. You feel like you're the only one who is struggling this way.

It can be *embarrassing*. Especially for Americans, who place a strong emphasis on financial success. When your career goes down the tubes, so does your self-esteem. In this book, I'm not going to dwell much on the emotional fallout of a recession. The psychological part is just not where my talents lie. I will share one bit of advice, though. It's something that my mother has told me many times: *be kind to yourself*. In a recession, being kind to yourself means taking to heart the fact that there are lots of people who are experiencing the same thing. You're not alone, and it's not your fault. But you *can* do something about it.

HOW DO I KNOW WHEN A RECESSION IS COMING?
Talking heads on the TV go on and on about "the economy." But what the heck does that even mean? "The economy" can feel like an abstract, unreal, made-up thing. In fact, the economy is very real, and it can help and hurt you in tangible ways. So having some basic understanding of how it works is just a non-negotiable part of being a responsible adult. A recent survey shows that the number one thing that both women and men want to accomplish in life is financial security.

You're not going to accomplish that without some basic economic literacy.

When it comes to making sense of the economy, many people suffer from "analysis paralysis." The economy seems to be a blur of numbers and data. The more you get into it, the more overwhelmed you get, and the less sense it makes. But I have good news for you: it's not as hard as it looks if you know what data matters most. The truth is that anyone can do it. All you need is an Internet connection and a little expert guidance on where to look. Ignore the noise. Here are the *only* numbers you need to pay attention to in order to predict an economic downturn:

1. The ISM Manufacturing Index
ISM stands for the Institute of Supply Management. They are an important organization that keeps an eye on what purchasing managers — the people at American companies who are in charge of buying things — are buying, and how confident they feel that they should be buying things. The ISM's Manufacturing Index captures those sentiments for the manufacturing sector. In simple terms, it's a number that tells you how well the American manufacturing industry is performing. Now, manufacturing is a small part of the U.S. economy — it's only 13 percent.

Here's the thing, though: the manufacturing sector leads the total U.S. economy in terms of growth. In other words, if the U.S. manufacturing sector contracts and falls into recession, you can bet that the entire U.S. economy is not too far behind. In fact, to prove this point, I've included Figure 2-2, which shows the ISM Manufacturing Index over time. This graph includes bars showing past recessions.

Based on the historical trend of the ISM Manufacturing Index over the past 65 years, declines below 50 are a good leading indicator of U.S. recession, with declines below 40 providing an almost guarantee that a recession is underway. In other words, if you want to predict the timing of the next recession, watch the ISM Manufacturing Index.

The ISM Manufacturing Index is the most important indicator out there, by far. It is everything. If you watch nothing else, watch that.

You can get it for free here: www.instituteforsupplymanagement.org/ismreport/mfgrob.cfm

Figure 2-2: ISM Manufacturing Index[2]

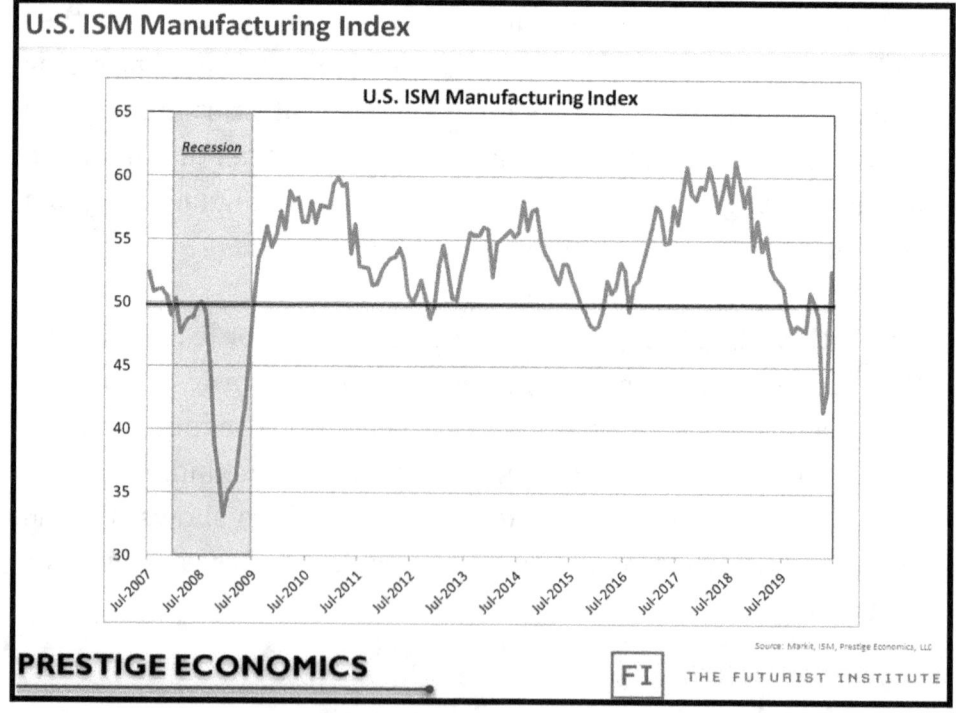

Set up a Google Alert so that you can see this number whenever it is released. Reading and understanding the index is simple.

The ISM Manufacturing Index consists of a single number, expressed as a percentage. Fifty is the break-even point. Fifty means that the sector is neither growing nor contracting. If the number is above 50, it's growing. If it's below 50, it's contracting. As the manufacturing sector goes, so goes the rest of the economy. So if this number starts to inch — or plummet — towards 50, you know that manufacturing is grinding to a halt and the country is closing in on a recession. For instance, through March 2020, the ISM had been below 50 for six of eight months.

What does this tell you? It tells you that the U.S. manufacturing industry has slowed down significantly — and that it is already contracting. That means the U.S. economy as a whole is likely to do the same, very soon.

Why is this ISM number so important? It is important because it measures, among other things, *sentiment* — basically, how do the people in charge of buying things at companies *feel* about taking the risk of buying things? Now, you might ask, why should we care about *sentiment*; why should we care about what these people *feel*? We should care because they're making the decisions, they see the flow of materials, and they know what's coming for manufacturing — and the entire economy. They *see and feel* a slowdown coming first. If a company *feels* worried about where the economy is going, they're not going to take the risk of expanding. They're going to downsize and hunker down. So they won't grow and they won't be hiring.

If enough companies do this, guess what? People aren't getting jobs, companies aren't making money, and you've got a recession. So what they *feel* really matters.

If you want to up your game even more, you can keep track of the **Beige Book**. It's a report put out by the "Fed" — the Federal Reserve System — based on sentiment and activity information collected from executives, economists, and various business professionals about what is going on in their businesses and how optimistic they feel about where their businesses are headed. This information gets distilled into this report, and anyone can access it. It's another great source of "sentiment" information, although it is not in the form of a neat and clean index. Here is a link to the Federal Reserve Beige Book reports: http://www.federalreserve.gov/monetarypolicy/beigebook/

A very senior guy I know who works at the CIA is fond of saying that the plural of *anecdote* is *data*. He's absolutely right. That's what indexes of sentiment are — thousands of anecdotes of how optimistic different companies are about their business. When you put all those anecdotes together, you get some very powerful data on what the economy is doing. It's incredible the sort of access that anyone with an Internet connection can get to the most powerful businesspeople in the country.

You probably don't have the time or interest to talk to bankers and oil barons and CEOs all day. That's what *I* do. I'm at invitation-only Fed events. I personally attend OPEC meetings. I go to closed-door dinners. I meet almost every year with the European Central Bank and the Bank of England.

That's what I do. That's what economists do. We do it so that you don't have to. Some of the most important information is passed on to you in the form of indexes, and, amazingly, they can be accessed for free.

2. The Fed's Policy Interest Rates

The "Fed" is the Federal Reserve System. It's the United States' central bank. Basically, its job is to even out the business cycle — the up-and-down movement of the economy. It can't do away with the business cycle, but it can make the highs not so manic and the lows not so depressed.

How does it do that? It does that by controlling the interest rate. The interest rate can be understood as the "price of money." It's how much money you have to pay (in interest) to *get* money (take out a loan) in order to invest in something.

When interest rates are low, money is cheap—so people want to take out loans, and use that money to start businesses, invest in the stock market, or buy a house. When interest rates are high, money is expensive, and people are more wary of spending or borrowing it.

They're not going to take out loans unless they're really, *really* sure that their investment is going to pay off. In a nutshell, what the Fed typically does is *raise* interest rates when the economy is on an upswing (to cool things off and prevent inflation), and then it lowers interest rates when the economy is doing poorly (to heat things up and encourage people to invest, which leads to growth).

So it's the Fed's business to predict — and influence — when the next recession is going to come. If anyone should know what's going to happen, it's them, and they employ *gaggles* of economists to figure that out. They're not always right, but they make important policies that impact growth, so they should definitely be listened to. Interpreting what the Fed is doing isn't that hard. Watching for Fed interest rate cuts is most important, because the Fed can raise interest rates even if growth is not fantastic, if it wants to kill inflation. Fed interest rate cuts mean the economy is slowing.

The other thing to watch are the Fed statements, which are short written reports that accompany Fed decisions about interest rates. If the Fed is concerned about the economy in its statement, you should be concerned. If the Fed is confident about the economy in its statement, you should feel confident. That's all you need to know.

Here is a link to all of the Fed's statements, calendars, and even their own forecasts of growth, inflation, and interest rates that they publish once per quarter. http://www.federalreserve.gov/monetarypolicy/fomccalendars.htm

3. The U.S. Unemployment Rate

The third thing to pay attention to is the U.S. unemployment rate. For most readers of this book, this is the number that has the most direct impact on your life. Your personal recession is usually about losing your job and not being able to find another one. So the percentage of U.S. workers who are looking for, but can't find, work is super-important.

There are plenty of details here, like "unemployment" vs. "underemployment," and "shadow employment," and "labor force participation," and so forth, but don't worry too much about that. Just look at the overall unemployment number, and notice the trend.

A one-month rise is nothing to fret over, but if the unemployment rate goes up four months in a row, that's a bad sign. In fact, it's *really* bad, because the unemployment rate tends to lag the business cycle. By the time the unemployment rate begins rising significantly, the entire economy could already be in recession. Pain in the labor market tends to continue even after a recession is over. This makes it really important to notice a rise in the unemployment rate early.

The numbers are all here, in the U.S. Bureau of Labor Statistics' reports: http://www.bls.gov/bls/proghome.htm

USING THE NUMBERS

That's it. Those are the only three numbers you need to look at. Don't bother poring over every little economic indicator. Don't bother listening to the 24/7 pundits on CNBC, Bloomberg, and Fox Business (well, unless it's me, of course). The truth is that they need to keep people tuned in every day, so they'll make mountains out of molehills. Ignore the noise, and just pay attention to those key indicators. By the way, the GDP — the Gross Domestic Product — is one of those numbers you don't need to pay attention to. That might sound strange, since it measures the value of everything that the country is producing. But really, the GDP is "Zeus on high." It's way off in the distance.

What matters to you, what can help or hurt you, is the job market. Besides, GDP numbers are revised so much that the actual data is published almost *six months* after the fact. That's too late! GDP is very backward-looking, while the three indicators that I've told you about are more forward-looking — especially the ISM Manufacturing Index.

Look ahead of you, not behind you. I hope you can see now that the economy isn't as complicated and mysterious as it first appears.

Another way to put it is this: the economy *is* extremely complicated and mysterious, but thousands of extremely smart, highly trained wonks are constantly measuring every imaginable aspect of it, and putting all of these measurements together into handy numbers that distill all of the important information. Then they give out those numbers for free to anyone who wants them. If you know the right numbers to watch, you won't need an economist to have a good sense of when the next recession is going to hit. Let me give you some examples of how individuals might use these numbers to their advantage.

A college student.

Let's say that you are a student in college. What do these numbers mean to you, and how can you act on them? First, some bad news. People like you are the hardest hit in an economic downturn. The crap runs downhill and it plops right on you. To avoid this, your number one priority must be to *graduate into a job*.

This is incredibly important. However important you think it is, multiple that by five. If you don't graduate into a job — if you end up working for low wages just to make ends meet while you're waiting for a good job to come around — you haven't just made things harder for yourself right now, you've actually made things harder for yourself for the *rest of your life*. There is a very tragic phenomenon called *unemployment scarring*, which refers to the fact that taking a low-paying job when you're young will reduce your pay for the entire rest of your career. Your starting point is low, so even with yearly raises, you'll still make far less money than you would have if you had started out in a well-paying job.

The longer you're unemployed, the deeper the scarring will be.

VIEWS ON UNEMPLOYMENT SCARRING
"The gain from finding a job is significantly smaller than the initial harm from losing a job. This suggests a scar effect of job loss that lingers over time, one that even reemployment does not fully correct." CRISTOBAL YOUNG, STANFORD UNIVERSITY[3]

"Unemployment can exact a big personal toll on young people. Failure to find a first job or keep it for long can have damaging long-term consequences on their lives and career prospects." HANAN MORSY, INTERNATIONAL MONETARY FUND[4]

"A recession, therefore, should not be thought of as a one-time event that stresses individuals and families for a couple of years. Rather, economic downturns will impact the future prospects of all family members, including children, and will have consequences for years to come." JOHN IRONS, ECONOMIC POLICY INSTITUTE[5]

Figure 2-3 illustrates the impact of losing a job and unemployment scarring on future earnings.

So, you *must* graduate into a job. How do you do that? Well, one thing you can do is: try to be born in the right year. Unfortunately, no one decides when they're born. So that's not a great strategy.

Here's something that is actually doable: if you weren't born in the right year, at least *graduate* in the right year. That means graduating into a healthy economy, and that requires *knowing where you are in the business cycle.*

Figure 2-3: Unemployment Scarring

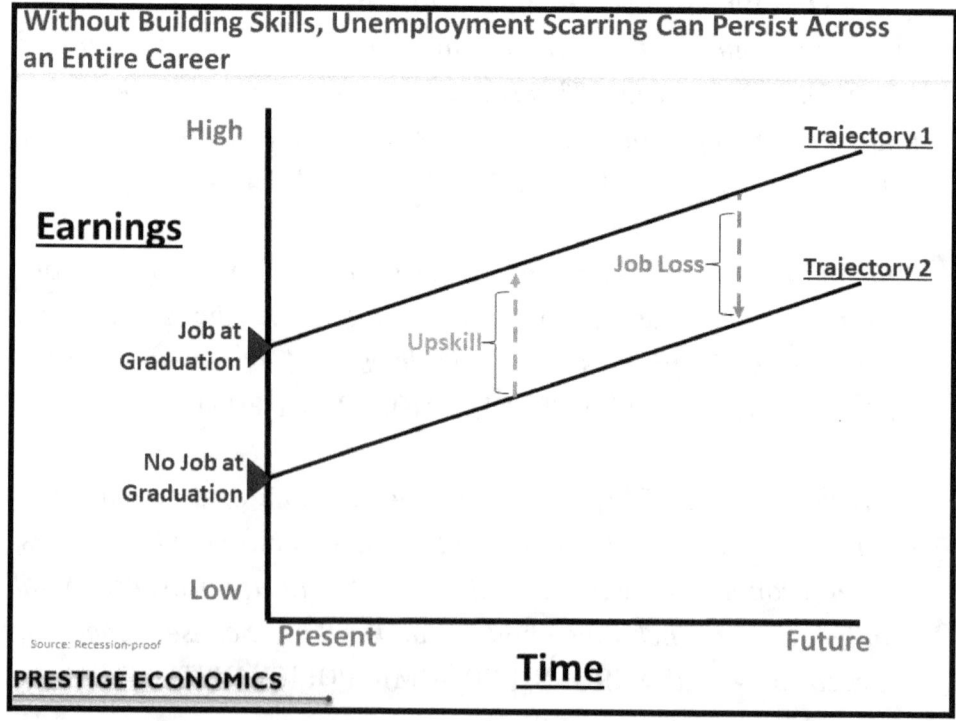

Look at those numbers.

Is the ISM Manufacturing Index falling towards 50, or even below it? Is the Fed starting to lower interest rates? Is the unemployment rate climbing? Don't graduate now! Do that Master's in Sociology, get an MBA, stay on for a fifth year of undergrad and become a "super-senior."

Wait it out, and then, when the economy is picking up, graduate into a job. Or, more rosily, is the ISM Manufacturing Index rising above 50? Is the Fed starting to gently raise interest rates? Is the unemployment rate dropping?

Time to graduate.

Finish up your courses as soon as you can, and don't go to graduate school. (Don't think that second dumbest thought I ever had.) Get a job now while the getting's good. An even better strategy in a good economy is to line up a job months before you graduate to lower your risks. After all, the cycle can change quickly.

Remove your risk by locking in a gig as soon as possible. If you're getting this advice too late — if you bought this book after the economy tanked and you just graduated into a lousy economy, and you are unemployed and living with your parents like so many other people your age — don't give up! Just get a job as soon as you possibly can, because the longer you're unemployed, the worse the unemployment scarring becomes. To get a job in a bad economy, you have to be *hungry*.

You need to know what educational opportunities, programs, or degrees would help you avoid becoming a dot in Figure 2-4.

A mid-career professional with kids in school.

You've got plenty on your plate. People are depending on you. So look at those numbers. Is the Fed putting the brakes on the economy? Is the Manufacturing Index tanking? A recession is coming, and you don't want to be its victim. Have a backup plan. *You need to know five to 10 people you could call right now to get a job.* If you don't know those five to 10 people, and have their numbers on speed dial, you're in trouble. The recession is going to hit you and your family hard.

Figure 2-4: Living at Home with Parents[6]

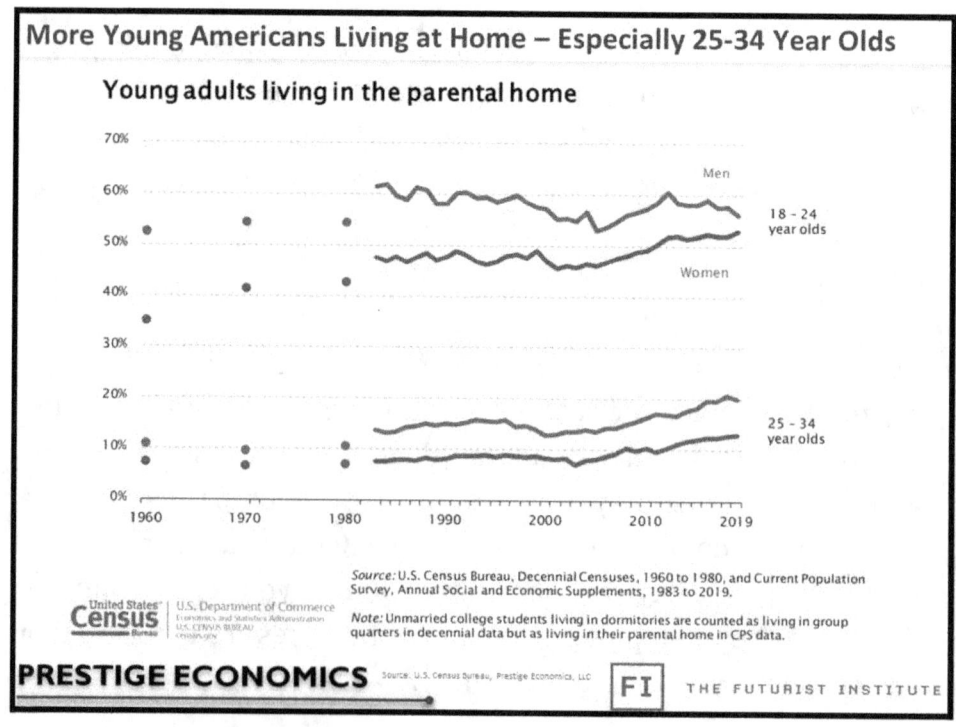

DRILL #2: TAKE STOCK OF YOUR EDUCATION OPPORTUNITIES

List 5 to 10 educational options you have to build your skills and wait out a recession.

1. _____

2. _____

3. _____

4. _____

5. _____

6. _____

7. _____

8. _____

9. _____

10. _____

Keep your resume updated and always ready.

This is a surprising roadblock for many people. You should be ready at any moment to jump into your next job. Be active on LinkedIn. Keep training. Keep your skills fresh. Meet people. Network outside your company.

You should be doing this all the time, but if the ISM Manufacturing Index just dropped below 50, you need to do it *now* — *today.* Put down this book and get on the phone. You need to know who could get you a job in a downturn — who could help you bridge that gap, so you and your family don't suffer.

You need these names.

If you don't have them, you need to make this your top professional priority.

A blue-collar worker.

If unemployment numbers are worsening — even if the ISM Manufacturing Index is healthy and the Fed is convinced that things are going fine — I've got bad news for you. Automation is swooping down on you.

Even if your company is doing well and growing, it is still going to cut jobs as automation advances. In other words, even if the United States never has another recession (which is *very, very, very, very, very unlikely*), your job is still in mortal danger. The machines are coming for your job right now.

DRILL #3: TAKE STOCK OF YOUR NETWORK

List 5 to 10 people you could call right now for a job tomorrow.

1. _____

2. _____

3. _____

4. _____

5. _____

6. _____

7. _____

8. _____

9. _____

10. _____

Here are just a few examples of where humans are being replaced with machines:

- Building things on factory lines
- Moving materials around a warehouse
- Booking hotel reservations, car rentals, and food delivery
- Taking orders at fast food restaurants
- Collecting bridge tolls
- Checking out customers at a grocery store

I've been to restaurants where you don't order from a server; you order from an iPad.

Amazon has been toying with the idea of delivering its products with flying drones.

Google and other companies are developing self-driving cars that could put cabbies and truckers out of business in the next decade.

The basic reason why companies go for automation is simple. Machines, computers, and robots can do a lot of physical labor for less money than a person. Unlike humans, they don't need healthcare. They're not entitled to overtime pay. They don't take a lunch break. They don't get injured and collect workers' compensation. They don't form unions. They don't go on strike.

Imagine a self-driving delivery truck — it could drive 24 hours a day, without sleep, without bathroom breaks, without meals, and cross the country in half the time or less than it would take a human driver.

The threat is real. But you've got some options. You can switch industries to one that is less vulnerable to automation. Anything that still involves empathy, people skills, customer-service finesse, or creative problem-solving is not likely to be automated any time soon.

If you have those "soft" skills, use them. If you don't, get them. ASAP.

You can invest in your education. Don't fear the machines; understand them. Get trained to *run* those machines. If you become the person who maintains, controls, and installs those machines, then automation won't hurt you. It will help you. If you're working on a factory line, get cross-trained in different things. You want to be the guy who knows how to run the computer that runs the machine that runs the line.

If you don't know how to run the machine that runs the line, it's only a matter of time before you lose your job. If the numbers say a recession is coming, you might even lose it tomorrow. The time to upskill is now.

The total number of U.S. manufacturing jobs has been falling since the late 1970s. In recessions, the losses add up quickly, and they don't recover much during the boom years.

As automation rises and machines replace people in large numbers, this downward trend in manufacturing will probably get steeper. You need to know how to build your skillset now — easily, quickly.

DRILL #4: TAKE STOCK OF YOUR OPTIONS

List 5 to 10 things you could be cross-trained on at work or you would be interested in learning more about through an in-person or online class.

1. _____

2. _____

3. _____

4. _____

5. _____

6. _____

7. _____

8. _____

9. _____

10. _____

CHAPTER SUMMARY

- Recessions come in many forms.

- Pay attention to the Fed statements, unemployment rates, and most importantly, the ISM Manufacturing Index, because they reflect the health of the economy and job market.

- You need people to call in case of a downturn.

- The goal is to have options.

CHAPTER 3

YOU HAVE OPTIONS

YOU, INC.
Some people think there's nothing they can do when a recession hits. Either they get lucky and do fine, or they get unlucky and suffer, but either way it's out of their hands.

But here's the funny thing. If you ask these same people, "Well, what can a *business* do when a recession is coming?" they can name plenty of things. Downsize, rebrand, relocate, and so forth.

So my question to you is: if a business has options, why wouldn't *you*? The truth is you do have options — and those options are fundamentally similar to the options that a company has. Think of yourself as a business. You have your revenue (your income), your investors (your parents), your assets (your house, your car, your vinyl LP collection), your overhead (all your living expenses), your human resources (your education and skills), and your all-important stockholders to whom you must deliver value (your spouse, your kids, yourself). So, the same tools that businesses use to understand their situations are ones that you can use, too.

DRILL #5: THE SWOT ANALYSIS

The SWOT analysis is a tool used by businesses, executives, and MBAs to think about how to handle challenging situations. SWOT stands for Strength, Weaknesses, Opportunities, and Threats. It's become a standard exercise for companies big and small, and even for government agencies and charities. All of these organizations use it because it's a comprehensive way of looking at everything good and everything bad in a situation. The great thing about a SWOT analysis is how balanced it is. It includes both positive aspects (Strengths, Opportunities) and negative aspects (Weaknesses, Threats) in a specific situation. Just as important, it includes both *internal* factors (Strengths, Weaknesses) and *external* factors (Opportunities, Threats). This balance is what makes it so good at uncovering aspects of your situation that you wouldn't initially think of.

For an individual, one thing that can be both a strength and a weakness is having a spouse with a stable job. This is a strength, because it lets you start your own business while depending on your spouse's income (see Chapter 8). It's also a weakness, because it prevents you from moving to where the jobs are (see Chapter 7). For a business, a SWOT analysis is supposed to be an objective, emotionless exercise. For an individual, a SWOT analysis can be intensely personal. Even so, it works best when you try to be as objective and honest with yourself as possible. Seeing things how they are — no matter how negative — can guide you towards a more successful path. Now let's do a SWOT analysis of You, Inc. The key here is to think not just about where you are now, but also where you're hoping to be in five, 10, or 20 years. Below is some guidance for each of the letters.

S: Strengths

It's the question you always get asked at a job interview: what are your biggest strengths? Your "hard" skills, like certifications and technical competencies, obviously count. List those. But don't forget to include the "soft" skills too. These include things like working well in teams, being able to charm potential clients, being approachable, being a good listener, reading people well, and so forth. Strengths also include the financial benefits of your household — for instance, having a spouse with a steady income. Also, if you are single with no kids, or have a spouse that likes to travel, or have young children whose social lives would not be disrupted by a move, that presents a great opportunity to relocate to a boom town.

List your five biggest personal or professional strengths that are important for your career:

Strengths (S)

1. _____

2. _____

3. _____

4. _____

5. _____

W: Weaknesses

It's the *other* question you always get asked at a job interview, the question you dread: what is your biggest weakness? In a job interview, you probably want to answer with a backhanded compliment, like "My biggest weakness is that I work too hard." But here, in the privacy of your own home, you can be more honest than that. What are you not so good at? Does the idea of giving a presentation in front of hundreds of people make you weak in the knees? Are you hopeless at math and computers? List it. There's no shame. I won't judge.

List your five biggest personal or professional weaknesses that hurt your career:

Weakness (W)

1. _____

2. _____

3. _____

4. _____

5. _____

O: Opportunities

Is there an industry, region, or country that is heating up right now? Are there training opportunities at your job that you could take advantage of? Could you stay in school with funding while furthering your education and building your skills?

List five external opportunities that could help your career:

Opportunities (O)

1. _____

2. _____

3. _____

4. _____

5. _____

T: Threats

Think back to Drill #1 in Chapter 2: what could come along and make your job go the way of the dodo? Is a national recession on the horizon? Is your state or county doing poorly? Are you in a recession-prone industry, like hotels? Is your job title getting a lot more common in Vietnam, and a lot less common in Virginia? Does your boss dislike you? Are robots doing your job at your company or at your competitors? These are all threats.

List five external threats that could hurt your career:

Threats (T)

1. _____

2. _____

3. _____

4. _____

5. _____

My SWOT analysis in 2001

Let me give you an example.

Below is what my SWOT analysis looked like in 2001. This was right when I finished my Master's degree in German, and was learning that, out in the real world, no one cares if you know the genitive case declination of the word *Schmetterling* or if you could read medieval German literature in its original.

That is especially true if, like me, you just had the second stupidest thought of your life, spent two years in graduate school, and reentered the job market at the worst possible time, like a chump.

Figure 3-1: My SWOT Analysis in 2001

SWOT	Positive	Negative
Internal	**Strengths** - Master's degree - Fluency in German - Strong grades and interest in economics - Willingness to do another degree - Freedom of movement (no spouse, no children)	**Weaknesses** - Few professional skills - Limited professional network - Academic track record without industry experience
External	**Opportunities** - Stay in graduate school for PhD	**Threats** - 2001 Recession

It wasn't a pretty picture. But looking at it through the SWOT lens, I could see positives as well as negatives. I managed to use my strengths to create opportunities and pull myself out of a bad situation. I used my fluency in German, strong grades, interest in economics, and freedom of movement to relocate and get another Master's degree, this time in Applied Economics, doing research in German on Austrian economics. I won't get into the details here, but the point is that if you go through the SWOT exercise, you'll see where your options are. In my own experience, your strengths and opportunities hold the key to moving forward. Putting all of your answers into a table like mine will help you see it more clearly.

Knowing your options: that's the most important thing of all. So let's look at the six basic chess moves that people like you can take in a recession, the six strategies that the SWOT analysis will help you choose between. Which strategy you end up using will depend on your specific situation and goals, but the basic alternatives are the same for everyone.

Strategy 1: Prepare (Chapter 4)
What does it mean? It means get your head in the game, get hungry, anticipate the next recession, build your resume, and ask yourself what you're willing to do when the chips are down, and what you're not. You're reading this book, so you've already taken a great first step toward preparing.

Who should do it? Everyone! This is the foundational step, and no matter your particular situation, you've got to do it.

Strategy 2: Dig In (Chapter 5)

What does it mean? This means doing everything possible to stay in your current job, company, or industry. It means clinging on like a barnacle. It means becoming that indispensable employee who keeps his or her job even when other people in the same situation are losing theirs.

Who should do it? This strategy is best for individuals who aren't able to change their life situations easily. If you're the sole breadwinner for your family, if you have an elderly parent to take care of, or if it's extremely important to you to stay in the town where you grew up and where all your friends and family live, then this is the option for you.

Strategy 3: Hide (Chapter 6)

What does it mean? This means taking refuge from the recession, either by staying in school (or going back to school) until the economy is looking up, or by finding a safe-haven job in a recession-proof industry.

Who should do it? It's easiest to go back to school if you're young, but, really, anyone can do it. As for finding a job in a recession-proof industry, that will depend on whether you have those skills. If you have chops in education, healthcare, and government, hunkering down in those stable sectors is a good option.

Additionally, technology has recently become a much more recession-proof industry — especially during the COVID-19 recession, when technology helped many people work remotely and kept their businesses operating.

Strategy 4: Run (Chapter 7)

What does it mean? It means physically relocating to a geographical location where prospects are better. It can also mean pivoting out of an industry or a company that is going down the tubes. It's about focusing on what you're running toward, not what you're running away from.

Who should do it? Moving physically is easiest if you are unencumbered. That often means that you're young and don't have a spouse or kids, but it might also mean that you and your spouse are empty nesters looking for a new adventure.

Strategy 5: Build (Chapter 8)

What does it mean? It means two things: build your skills, or build your own business.

Both of them are investments in You, Inc. And they can provide long-term value to your career and business long after a recession has ended.

Who should do it? Everyone can build their skills. As for building a business, it's generally best for someone with a long runway — the amount of time you can afford to spend building your business before it turns a profit.

People with long runways tend to be people who either have a spouse who makes a steady income, people who have a chunk of money in the bank that they can afford to lose, or people who have various assets they can sell off to finance their entrepreneurial adventure.

Strategy 6: Invest (Chapter 9)

What does it mean? It means putting money into an existing business to grow it, helping pay for your kids' education, or investing very, very carefully in the stock market. It doesn't mean buy and selling individual stocks — unless you *really* know what you're doing.

Who should do it? Anyone with kids should absolutely be investing in their education, not just for their sake but for your sake!

You'll depend on them when you're older. Anyone with some money in the bank should put it into a safe mutual fund. Only the brave, the savvy, or the foolish will engage in active trading.

CHAPTER SUMMARY

- You are a business: You, Inc.

- Know your SWOT.

- Assess your options.

- Your strengths and opportunities hold the key to moving forward.

CHAPTER 4

PREPARE

GET IN THE GAME

First things first: surviving and thriving during a recession isn't easy, but you can do it. Plus, the earlier you start, the easier it is.

You want to recession-proof your life sooner rather than later. You have a big advantage on your side: you have the benefit of foresight. Remember those indicators I told you about in Chapter 1? The magical thing about those indicators is that they don't just tell you that a recession is already happening; they can help you *predict* it before it happens. For instance, the ISM Manufacturing Index falls below 50 *before* an economic slowdown really hits. So you know that it's coming before it's here.

This is your goal in this chapter. Get mentally in the game. Be alert, pay attention, and think strategically, even before the recession has hit. It's like hitting the gym before a big game. Here's how to get in shape now, so that you're lean and mean when the economic you-know-what hits the fan.

WEIGH YOUR OPTIONS

The first thing to do is to complete this chapter's drills. They are longer than the other drills in this book, and they might take you a good 15 minutes to do thoroughly, but trust me, it's absolutely necessary. You can think of it as a different take on the SWOT analysis — looking at what threatens you as well as what you want to accomplish. Most of it is pretty self-explanatory, but here are a few tips to get the most out of it.

A recession is an opportunity.

Some of the items in the "What are my goals?" section might sound unrealistic or even delusional when you're looking down the barrel of a recession. How can I possibly afford to own a dream home or travel around the world when the economy is doing poorly? How can I start a successful company when no one's buying anything? Who has time to learn another language or do something selfless when I'm struggling just to make ends meet?

This line of thinking is completely backwards. Believe it or not, a recession can be the *best* time to do all these things, and the *easiest* time to make them happen.

Let's take each skeptical question in turn.

"How can I possibly afford to own a dream home or travel around the world when the economy is doing poorly?" Let's turn that question on its head. How could you possibly afford to buy a house or go traveling when the economy is doing *well*?

In up years, everyone wants to buy a house and the real estate sector goes nuts. It becomes a seller's market. Just ask anyone who tried to buy a house in San Francisco in the middle of the dot-com bubble in the late '90s. It sounds like the best time to buy, but it's actually the worst. Any financial advisor will tell you to buy low and sell high. When it comes to buying a house, that means: buy during a recession. If you can swing it financially, this is the time to do it.

As for traveling, remember that tourism, leisure, and hospitality are industries that are exceptionally vulnerable to a recession. When people have less money, they're going to cut back on these luxuries. That means that in down years, hotel rooms and plane tickets get much cheaper. If you have some money tucked away for that round-the-world adventure you've always dreamed of, a recession is the perfect time to get maximum bang for your buck. When the economy stinks, what are you giving up in order to do that? Not much.

"How can I start a successful company when no one's buying anything?"

Simple: because when no one's buying anything, stuff is cheap. When stuff is cheap, your start-up costs for a business are low. By the time the economy picks up again, your business will be ready to rock. I'll give you the full scoop on this in Chapter 9.

"Who has time to learn another language or do something selfless when I'm struggling just to make ends meet?"

Again, turn the question on its head: who can afford *not* to be building their skills through education and volunteering at a time when you need to stand out from the crowd of other applicants? Learning another language isn't just a hobby; it's a resume-builder and it shows employers that you're still growing, learning, and hustling. Volunteering for your community isn't just a good deed; it's a great opportunity to gain professional experience in a new field. Since you're not being paid, it's easy to get the organization to say yes to "hiring" you. Then, with that experience under your belt, you're poised to get a job doing that same thing *for money*. More about this in Chapters 5 and 8.

There's a concept in economics called *opportunity cost*. Basically, it's what you give up in order to get something. If you adopt a cat, you have direct costs like cat food, vet bills, etc. You also have opportunity costs: all the things that you can't do now that you have a cat, like leave town at a moment's notice, or invite your allergic mother over, or have an open tank full of goldfish in the living room. Just as other costs go down during a recession, so do opportunity costs. If no one's hiring, what do you have to lose by taking a few months off for that trip to Colombia you've always dreamed of? Nothing. If you're out of work, what are you giving up when you decide to spend your time learning Japanese and volunteering for the Red Cross? Nothing.

Low opportunity costs are one of the big reasons why a recession isn't just a threat, it's an opportunity. If you were always itching to try out a new city, a new career, a new hobby — really, any change at all — a recession is the time to do it.

Your career is a sculpture.

When you do Drill #7 in this chapter, the "negative" questions (What am I *not* willing to do? What do I *not* like?) are also very important. I had a career counselor when I was finishing my undergrad in 1999. One of her greatest kernels of wisdom was this: your career is a sculpture. When you're figuring out what to do with your life, you're like a sculptor who starts out with a big block of rock. That block of rock is all your possible careers — plumber, pilot, pianist, and everything else. How does a sculptor work? Not by adding things, but by taking things away, until the only thing remaining is what should be there. When you go out into the world, try a job out, and decide it's not for you, you're chiseling a piece off of that block. If you do that enough times, you're left with all the things you *do* like and *are* good at. That's your sculpture; that's your career. That's why those "negative" questions are so important.

Of course, looking back, I sometimes wish that career counselor had just told me to get a job while the economy was hot. If she had told me that, maybe I wouldn't have fallen prey to the second dumbest thought I ever had.

Downsizing is an option.

In the "What am I willing to do?" section of Drill #7, one of the possibilities is "downsize my expenses." Now, I wrote this book to help you *avoid* that situation where you have to downsize. But if all else fails, downsizing is an option.

Housing is often the best place to cut your costs. Whether you're living a five-figure lifestyle or a seven-figure lifestyle, your biggest cost is probably your housing. You can massively reduce that cost by moving in with relatives or living with roommates. That's not always the most pleasant option, but it does come at a huge savings to you.

For some people, the idea of downsizing may even be attractive. Maybe you've recently become an empty-nester. Your last kid just left for college and you're tired of having three bathrooms to clean, and you are looking forward to trading in that old, musty family home in the suburbs for a sleek new condo in the city. Whatever your situation and your priorities, you need to ask yourself what downsizing might look like and how far you're willing to take it.

Remember: you're a business — You, Inc. When recessions come, businesses cut costs, and you can do the same. The most successful businesses don't just freak out when the recession comes and cut everything — they plan ahead and cut smartly. You should do the same. Ask yourself: Do I need that new BMW, or is last year's Toyota just fine? Do I actually need or want this five-bedroom, three-bathroom home that I bought to house my kids who have now flown the coop? If I telecommute, do I actually need to live in this expensive city, or can I move somewhere more affordable without sacrificing my job? Notice that I wrote "downsizing your expenses," not "downsizing your life." Reducing costs doesn't mean reducing your standard of living.

When I founded Prestige Economics, I was living in Houston. I often travel long distances for work, so where I live doesn't actually make that much difference to my career. So I decided to move to a city with higher bang-for-your-buck. I relocated to Austin, Texas and I've never looked back. Overnight my housing costs and the price of my car insurance were cut in half. I was living just as rich a lifestyle, but spending less money for it.

DRILL #6: Rank your Risks

Rank the following risks to your livelihood, from most to least risky on a 10 point scale, with 10 the most and 1 the least:

BOSS RISK (DOES YOUR BOSS NOT LIKE YOU?)
Least — 1 2 3 4 5 6 7 8 9 10 — Most

ECONOMY RISK (IS THE ECONOMY ABOUT TO TANK?)
Least — 1 2 3 4 5 6 7 8 9 10 — Most

INDUSTRY RISK (IS YOUR INDUSTRY GOING DOWNHILL?)
Least — 1 2 3 4 5 6 7 8 9 10 — Most

REGION RISK (IS YOUR REGIONAL ECONOMY WEAK?)
Least — 1 2 3 4 5 6 7 8 9 10 — Most

COMPANY RISK (IS YOUR COMPANY FAILING?)
Least — 1 2 3 4 5 6 7 8 9 10 — Most

AUTOMATION RISK (IS YOUR JOB GOING TO A MACHINE?)
Least — 1 2 3 4 5 6 7 8 9 10 — Most

REPLACEABILITY RISK (IS SOMEONE WHO WILL WORK FOR LESS MONEY GOING TO BE HIRED IN YOUR PLACE?)
Least — 1 2 3 4 5 6 7 8 9 10 — Most

SCORING YOUR RISK

Now add up all of the numbers: _____
• If you have less than 25 points total, your risks are low. Secure your position further by following the steps outlined below.

• If you have 26 to 40 points, your risks are balanced. The good news is that things are probably going pretty well right now. The bad news is that your job could become at risk quite quickly in an economic downturn. Secure your position further
by following the steps outlined below.

• If you have more than 40 points, your risks are high. Move through this book as quickly as possible, and stay in close contact with the 5 to 10 people you could call for a job.

Now look at how many categories there are that you scored a 9 or 10 in:
• If you scored a 9 or 10 in one category, your risks are high, and your position could be in jeopardy soon.

• If you scored a 9 or 10 in two or more categories, your risks are very high, and the elimination of your position could be imminent.

I hope that didn't scare you. But if it did, all the more reason to get in gear *now*. To help you see the opportunities — not just the risks — take a closer look at yourself than the SWOT analysis allowed.

DRILL #7: KNOW THYSELF

Now that you know the risks to your current job, let's think proactively. The following questions are designed to help you identify what you like and dislike about your job, your long-term goals, and what you are willing to do to get there. Even if your job risk is low, you should still consider the possibilities and whether or not you're truly content.

What are 5 to 10 things I like about my job?

1. _____

2. _____

3. _____

4. _____

5. _____

6. _____

7. _____

8. _____

9. _____

10. _____

What are 5 to 10 things I don't like about my job?

1. _____

2. _____

3. _____

4. _____

5. _____

6. _____

7. _____

8. _____

9. _____

10. _____

What are my goals?

Circle which of the following you would like to accomplish in the next five years:

- Be financially secure.
- Have a family.
- Get married.
- Travel around the world.
- Own a dream home.
- Have a successful career.
- Do something selfless.
- Live abroad.
- Learn another language.
- Start your own company.

What am I willing to do in a recession?

Am I willing to…

…move to a new city?	Yes	No
…move to a new country?	Yes	No
…switch companies?	Yes	No
…change job function?	Yes	No
…change industries?	Yes	No
…go back to school?	Yes	No
…downsize my expenses?	Yes	No
…change careers?	Yes	No
…stick it out at my current job?	Yes	No

Was there anything that surprised you about this drill?

Is there something missing from your life or career?

Is there something you would—and could—change about your current job?

The onset of recession could present opportunities to explore those options.

And that's one of the most important things to keep in mind when faced with recession: you have options.

Sometimes those options fall in your lap, and sometimes you have to scurry to make those options become viable realities. But if you stay agile and push forward, you are likely to have more options than if you let yourself be a victim of a fate that seems imminent.

BE THE FIRST RAT OFF THE SHIP

Let me give you a few other pieces of wisdom as you look ahead to the next economic downturn. If you have a job in a company that is going to be hard hit when the recession comes, *get out sooner rather than later*.

There are several good reasons for this. One of those reasons is this: The first rats off the sinking ship make it into the life raft.

The last rat gets nada.

So, if your company is starting to lay people off, be the one who leaves early, with a Voluntary Separation Package, or VSP. People sometimes call a VSP a golden handshake: it can be as much as an entire year's salary. A lot of companies start offering them when they know that the economy is slowing down and layoffs are coming. They essentially give you money to go away.

So take it. Take the buyout and move on, while you still have options.

Another reason to take the deal is that the people who stay at a company while it's downsizing often end up pretty miserable. They're carrying the workload of all those people who left before them, plus they're constantly worried about losing their job.

There's a scene in the movie *Glengarry Glen Ross* where Alec Baldwin chews out a room full of real estate salesmen with a famously harsh speech. He tells them to close those sales. First prize is a new Cadillac. Second prize is a set of steak knives.

Third prize is you're fired.

That's what it feels like if you stick around a company that's doing some serious downsizing. Actually, it's worse: first prize is a set of steak knives, second prize is you're fired. That's why, in a 10,000-person layoff or VSP offering, you don't want to be body number 981, or 2,350. You want to be body number one. Let me put it this way: you really, *really* didn't want to be the last middle manager working at Blockbuster.

I'll bet you any amount of money that he or she did not get a good severance package. I can also tell you for sure that the writing was on the wall many, many months, or even years, before he or she got axed. There's a twist here, though. When companies know they have to downsize, they'll hand out those VSPs — those golden handshakes or golden parachutes — to the *worst* workers first. If you're a really good worker, they don't want to lose you, so they'll try to keep you on. Then, when you finally get thrown to the curb at the lowest point in the recession, you get a lousy VSP or none at all, *and* you're plopped on the job market at the toughest possible time.

Meanwhile, your lower-performing colleagues got golden handshakes *and* hit the job market before the economy really tanked. No good deed goes unpunished. So if you missed your opportunity for a golden handshake, don't feel bad.

It may actually reflect well on you.

This goes in the category of *be kind to yourself*.

But just because it's not your fault, doesn't mean you couldn't have avoided it. Get out early. You want to have something else lined up before you bail, but don't be afraid to make the jump early.

How do you know when your company is going the way of the Titanic? I already told you one: if your colleagues are getting golden handshakes and bolting, that's a sign. If the company isn't hiring, that's a sign. If salaries have been frozen, that's a sign.

If the company's top performers are struggling to attract money and contracts and clients to the firm, that's a sign. At the beginning of 2009, I was at McKinsey, the huge management consulting firm, working out of their Houston office.

I could tell things were drying up.

At a firm like that, what matters to the bosses is how many billable hours you're working per day. You might work hard from 7:00 a.m. to 11:00 p.m., but if none of those were billable hours, that meant that no clients were paying for your work, so you didn't bring even a single cent to the company. Well, in Quarter 1 of 2009, I was averaging just one or two billable hours a day, yet that still made me one of the top performers for billable hours!

This is the kind of sign I'm talking about. If you're a top performer at a global leading company and you're essentially working just one hour a day, it's time to get out. Your company is going down.

BEEF UP YOUR RESUME

One way to counter the downside risks of recession is to focus on your education. And education does not end with school.

Take a continuing education class. If your employer offers in-house training or a budget for other training, jump on it. Learn a language. Take pottery lessons. Anything is better than nothing.

Why? Because it's the ability to learn, not the mastery of specific skills, that employers are looking for.

You probably won't use Latin at a tech firm, but if you can learn Latin, you can definitely learn HTML. Especially if you're an older worker, you might need to show employers that an old dog *can* learn new tricks — and that you want to!

When I was doing my Master's degree in German, I was reading and translating *medieval German plays*. Let me tell you, that is not easy. Did I ever need to read a medieval German play when I was Chief Energy Economist at Wachovia Bank? No. But picking up a tough skill like that definitely looks good to someone who's hiring for a job that requires constant growth and learning and boundary-pushing.

Fill in those gaps before you're sitting at the job interview thinking, "Man, I wish I had learned X or taken online course Y or did professional designation Z." Have that all buttoned up before the recession comes. In the boom years, you need to make sure you set aside some time, effort, and money to keep building, keep growing, and keep investing in *you*.

LinkedIn Learning and The Futurist Institute.

Other really practical ways to take classes and learn is to take LinkedIn Learning courses or do professional certifications like the one offered by The Futurist Institute.

Whatever you do, the most important thing is to be preparing yourself for the next job you get by building up your professional skills or demonstrating your ability to learn new things.

GET HUNGRY

The early bird gets the worm. Scratch that: the early *and really hungry* bird gets the worm. Being hungry isn't about desperation. It's about desire and determination.

How hungry do you have to be?

Maybe *this* hungry: In 2001, after I had the second dumbest thought I ever had, I missed out on the boom years and graduated into a slump. Things weren't good for me. I was overeducated and under experienced. I used my strengths to earn a second Master's degree in 2003, in Applied Economics. Even with the Master's in economics, though, I was *still* having trouble getting a job. To get by, I was living off of student loans and taking some additional MBA classes. I was attending a million job fairs and networking like crazy, trying to find a career job. I was looking anywhere and everywhere.

One of the places I looked is one you might have heard of: Fuddruckers, the hamburger chain. Fuddruckers had a little promotion going. At the front of the restaurant, there was a fish bowl, and customers could drop their business cards into the fish bowl for a chance to win a free burger.

You know what I did?

You know how *hungry* for a job I was? I went into that fish bowl and fished out business cards and *started calling the people on the business cards.* Some might call it desperate. I call it hungry.

That's my working definition of being *hungry*: you see a fishbowl full of business cards, and instead of thinking, "Hey, I could win a free burger," you think, "*Those guys might hire me.*"

If you're not hungry enough to reach into a fishbowl full of people who are just hoping to get a burger and send them unsolicited emails asking for a job, then guess what? You're not hungry enough. I'm sorry, but you're just not there yet. In a recession, you probably won't get a job.

In the end, the fishbowl isn't how I got a job.

I got a job in another very hungry way. I interviewed for an internship at Wachovia with the Chief Economist, but I didn't get the gig. I think someone on the hiring committee saw my two Master's degrees and got worried that I just wanted to keep being a student forever. In any case, I didn't get the job, but I kept emailing that guy, constantly, until he finally hired me. He told me later that the reason he hired me was so that I'd stop emailing him!

That's how hungry you have to be. Be hungry and be persistent. I applied to over a thousand jobs before I got one. Wachovia had rejected me for a job, rejected me for a mere *internship* no less, but when I emailed them a few months later, just to check in, they hired me. Just because the well is dry now, don't be afraid to go back to it later.

We'll talk later about how to get that list of five to 10 people you could call right now who would give you a job.

Unfortunately, school can be a very bad place to build that list because everyone you know is either a student or an academic.

So, until you have that list, you've got to be hungry.

Really, really hungry.

BE ADAPTIVE

Above all, be adaptive. Be flexible. You don't have to be willing to do *anything*, but you have to be willing to do a *lot* of things.

Recessions take away options; counter this by creating options and keeping them open. In the next chapter, we'll look at one of those options: Digging in.

CHAPTER SUMMARY

- Recession-proof yourself to gain advantages.

- Get in the game.

- Build your resume, even in small ways.

- Ask yourself what you'll do and what you won't do.

- Get hungry.

- Just because the well is dry now, don't be afraid to go back to it later.

CHAPTER 5

DIG IN

THE BARNACLE STRATEGY

Your son is in the fifth grade, and you can't bear to separate him from his best friend. Your mother's gone from gray to white, and you're now chauffeuring her around town almost as much as she chauffeured *you* around town when you were 14. There's just one industry in your small town, and you're in it. The company you work at is your *Cheers*, the place where everyone knows your name, the place you actually look forward to going each day.

If this sounds at all like you, I've got bad news. Your options in a recession are limited. But they are not zero. It is still possible to brace yourself against the downturn, and you can do this without packing your bags for an unfamiliar city, without changing industries, without jumping ship to another company.

You may even be able to do it without changing your job title. This is the strategy to Dig In. It's about latching on, like a barnacle, and not letting go. For anyone who can't make big changes, this is your best bet.

THE FIRST RULE OF DIGGING IN

Lots of people ask me for advice on what to do in a recession. The first thing I always say is, "Don't get fired." I always go back to that scene in *Glengarry Glen Ross*. First prize is a Cadillac, second prize is steak knives, third prize is you're fired. If you're in a recession-prone industry (in the movie, the salesmen are in real estate, and that's *very* recession-prone), that's the situation that you'll probably be in. In this chapter, I'll be equipping you with some strategies to make sure you're getting the car, or at least the knives.

The first thing you need to appreciate is that your job doesn't just vanish. Somebody *decides* to downsize the company. Just like somebody *decides* to axe certain jobs and people, while keeping others. It comes back to sentiment and the balance of fear and greed, which I told you about in Chapter 1.

If the high-up corporate strategy people at your company are feeling nervous, it's going to be bad. If they're feeling *very* nervous, it's going to be *very* bad. But even if they're scared out of their minds, it's not as though they're going to lay off the entire workforce. They're going to be choosy. You want to be on the right side of that choosiness.

DIVERSIFY YOUR BOSS RISK

The first thing you need to do is think long and hard about your *boss risk*. Your boss risk is the risk that your boss will fire you or lay you off.

Everyone needs to think about boss risk because everyone has a boss. Even if you own your own company, you still have a boss — your clients. If they stop buying your product, guess what? They just fired you. Even if you're the CEO of a big company, and you are calling the shots on a lot of day-to-day things, you still have a boss — the shareholders. If they lose confidence in your ability to deliver value to them, wham, bang, you're fired. So boss risk is a real threat for everyone.

When you can't change cities, industries, or even companies — when you've decided that digging in is your best or only option — your boss risk is especially high. That's because it's *undiversified*. You've just got one boss. A CEO has an entire board of directors who might like or dislike him. A small business owner has multiple customers. But if you're stuck in a single job, you've got just one boss. If he decides he doesn't like you, or if he turns out to be a turkey, you're gone. It's a sad truth that there are lots and lots of people in management positions who have no idea how to manage people. This presents some real boss risk.

Having just one boss is as risky as investing all your savings in a single stock. You need to be extra careful to anticipate if your boss — the *one* buffer between you and unemployment — has any reason to get rid of you. I'm not suggesting licking boots or putting an apple on your boss's desk every morning. But I am suggesting anticipating what that one reason to fire you might be, and heading it off early.

The only way to *really* diversify your boss risk is to start your own business and have many clients (see Chapter 8).

If you're committed to staying at your current company, though, you can still diversify your boss risk in smaller ways. Network within the company. Make friends, find allies, and build relationships. Remember that list of five to 10 people who you could call right now for a job? That list that everyone should have? Well, some of those names can be within your current company. If your company has an internal resume database, keep that resume fresh and updated. If you get transferred to a different department in your same company, that's a minimal disruption to your life, and no disruption at all to your kids in school, your spouse with the ailing father, or whatever else is tying you to your current circumstances.

It's always good to have these alternative jobs at your company lined up, even if you don't intend to use them. There's a famous negotiation book by Roger Fisher and William Ury called *Getting to Yes*. The book puts forward a very simple, but powerful, rule of negotiation: *whoever has options has power*. If you know someone else in the company would like to hire you, you will have more leverage in your current role. If you really don't like your current situation, you can just take the other job, and go work for that other boss. The more options you have, the better off you are — and the less crap you have to put up with.

BECOME INDISPENSABLE AT WORK

I've worked alongside a lot of day-traders, these folks who spend all day moving money in and out of five, six, and seven-figure positions. They like to say, "You need a million reasons to get into a trade. But you only need one reason to get out of a trade."

In a tough economic climate, the same is true of hiring and firing. You need a million skills on your resume to get a job, but you only need one missing skill to lose it. The trick is to make sure you have that skill — the skill that no one else has, the skill that makes you indispensable, the skill that makes you unfireable.

I offer a word of caution, though. In your quest to prove that you aren't just another employee, that you are an integral part of a company's workforce, you might step on some toes. You need to make sure to minimize the impact of this.

Let me give you an example. When I was working at McKinsey, the massive management consulting firm, I made sure to go above and beyond. I did special and sometimes extraordinary things. I appeared as an expert financial forecaster on television, on the radio, in print media, and at big conferences. This was basically unheard of at my company—especially for someone who was not at the director level. Inevitably, I ended up stepping on some toes. An old friend from my banking days invited me to give a high-profile keynote speech at a prestigious financial market conference, and one of the speakers on a smaller, less-visible panel at the same conference was one of the most senior people at McKinsey. He was a big shot who went on to work in the Obama administration, and he wasn't happy that a relatively new hire like me was getting the spotlight of a keynote. Luckily, he wasn't part of my reporting structure, and the people who I *did* report to were happy with the visibility. So take this as a warning. If you don't have options, don't rock the applecart with higher ups — even if they are in different departments.

DRILL #8: SKILLS TO LEARN

List 5 to 10 skills you could easily learn that might make you a more valuable new hire, or list 5 to 10 ways you could become more valuable in your current job in the next 3 months.

1. _____

2. _____

3. _____

4. _____

5. _____

6. _____

7. _____

8. _____

9. _____

10. _____

ALWAYS, ALWAYS, ALWAYS BE LEARNING

It's not about what you do when layoffs are already happening; it's about what you did during all those months and years leading up to that time. It's about that whole satchel of skills that you built up over time in your job.

Always be learning. If you're not learning, you're at a higher risk than you think. If you're not sharpening your tools, they're going to get rusty. Your education does not end with your Bachelor's, or even your Master's or MBA or PhD. You received your law degree and you think you're done? Wrong. You're not done.

You're never done. Luckily, there are lots of ways of adding to your skillset which cost you very little or nothing.

Get your company to pay for it.

Does your employer offer a budget for ongoing training? Use it. Milk that cow. Take full advantage of everything they offer, absolutely everything. If your company has a 401k matching program, do you take advantage of it?

Of course you do.

So why on earth would you not take advantage of their training budget? It's there for you to take. It comes back to what I talked about in the last chapter: *you've got to be hungry*. These opportunities might dry up in your company's leaner years, so grab them now while you can. If you're on a factory line, take advantage of cross-training, which is usually free.

Not many employers are going to say "no" to an employee who says, "Look, I just want to learn how to do the other stuff in the factory." Plus, it's those workers who end up becoming a floor manager, because they know how to do everything that the factory does.

Get a certification. There's been huge growth recently in the professional designation industry. I have a bunch of letters after my name, and so do most other serious professionals. You can think of these as signaling devices. They signal to your boss not just that you have knowledge, but that you also have drive, follow-through, ambition, and hunger. Just *enrolling* yourself in a certification program is good optics — even if it takes you many years to actually complete the program. Heck, even if you *never* complete the program! Merely being a *candidate* for a certification looks good, and you want to look good.

That being said, don't fake it. Don't enroll in a certification program that you have no intention of actually following. It will come back to haunt you. I knew a guy who had enrolled in the Chartered Financial Analyst (CFA) program but hadn't gotten around to actually learning any of the material. The CFA program is a very hard financial program. You can't fake it. By putting the enrollment on his resume before actually studying for it, he did himself a great disservice. He was in a job interview and they asked him an extremely basic question about bond ratings, and he didn't know the answer. He was caught in his lie. The interview was over at that moment. Don't get yourself in that situation. You don't need to know everything, but you need to know something.

THINGS YOUR CURRENT EMOLOYER MIGHT PAY FOR:

- Factory cross-training.
- Professional certifications.
- In-house training.
- Conference attendance.
- An MBA or other degree.

Your company may pay for you to attend a conference in order to market your company's products and network on their behalf. That's very common in the white collar world. Of course, while you're there, you can also be selling *you*, and networking with people who might want to hire *you*. This is a delicate thing — you don't want to spend all your time promoting yourself when your company is paying for you to promote *them* — but it is possible to walk that line.

Your company may even pay for you to do an entire degree. Do your research on what the options are. They may sponsor you to get an MBA. Once you've completed the degree, you might have to work a certain number of years for that company in order to clear your debt with them. That's called a "claw-back," but even a claw-back is usually a very good deal for you, because you pay nothing out of pocket. This kind of scheme is especially common at big consulting firms and public accounting firms. I even met a CEO who told me that he paid one of his staff to get a *PhD in Psychology*. When I was at McKinsey, they sent us off to an *Alpine chalet*. You don't know what your company will pay for until you look into it. You might be surprised by what you find.

Plus, you have nothing to lose. Any skill-building opportunities that your employer pays for or subsidizes is a great ROI — return on investment — for you. You'll carry that with you in your satchel whether you Dig In at your company or end up leaving.

Do it even when your company won't pay for it.

Now, I can hear you saying, "But my company is *too small* to pay for training!" Or, "My company *used to pay* for training, but now that the recession has hit, that ship has sailed." That's unfortunate, but it's not an excuse. Nowadays there is an infinite number of completely free, open-source, public-domain learning resources available with a simple Google search. There are online textbooks, webinars, and even educational YouTube videos online, which you can work through in the evenings.

Is there a particular computer program that you'd like to add to your resume? Download the free trial version. The 30 days you'll get with that product is more than enough to learn the basics. Then add it to your resume. To include that skill on your resume, you don't need to be the world's expert on that product. Unless that computer program is a critical component of a job, you probably just need to have a basic competence and familiarity with the program, since most companies will train you once you are hired.

Audit a class at your local university. That means showing up to the lectures without being enrolled. You don't get credit or a grade, but you do gain the knowledge, and you can list it on your resume.

At many universities, it's completely free. At others, there's a tiny fee.

At The University of Texas at Austin, my local university, it's just $20 to audit an entire class — and that's at one of the country's top public universities. If you want to build your business skills, an accounting class or a finance class could be a good option for you.

If you work for a multi-national company, even if you're working the assembly line, by all means learn one of the languages that your company uses. If you work in the United States for a foreign company, learn the home language. For example, if you work for Samsung, learn Korean, or if you work for BMW, learn German. Learning a language is a long and intense process, yes, but it doesn't need to be an *expensive* one.

All the grammar and vocabulary is on the web, 100 percent free. As for speaking practice, you don't need to hire a tutor or take an immersion class. Just sign up for a meetup group where Korean speakers practice their English with English speakers and vice-versa.

It's free, and fun. For any major world language in any major city, it's very likely that such a group exists. Showing interest in learning a relevant language will put you in line for a more senior position. Depending on how well you build your language skills, it could also make your resume stand out in the internal company database.

If you're prepared to shell out even a small amount of cash, your options multiply. Online courses are usually taken for a fee, but it tends to be a nominal one. Night classes at a local community college are generally a bargain, and are designed to accommodate busy people with 9-5 jobs. If there's an industry conference that you'd benefit from, but your company won't pay for you to go, ask them for unpaid time off to attend it on your own dime. Since it's not paid time off, you'll lose some wages, but you won't use up your precious paid vacation days.

Of course, attending a conference is not the cheapest option. It usually means paying for airfare, hotel, meals, conference registration, and so forth. Even so, it can offer you one of the highest ROIs. This is because a conference isn't just about learning, it's also about networking.

What a great networking opportunity it is, even — *especially* — during a recession. Last year I was invited to speak in Vancouver for the Institute of Scrap Recycling Industries. These are the companies that do things like crushing old cars into cubes and selling off the metal to be used again.

They're fully in recession right now because steel and other metal prices are so low. So, in a time when a lot of these companies are being squeezed, who has the time and money to fly to a national conference? The real players, that's who. It wasn't the folks who are having difficulties who came to the conference, it was the folks who are doing just fine.

THINGS YOU COULD DO AT LITTLE OR NO COST TO BECOME MORE INDISPENSABLE:

- Watch YouTube training videos.
- Attend webinars.
- Read online textbooks.
- Sign up for an online course.
- Take night classes.
- Audit a course at your local university.
- Download the free trial version of a software package.
- Attend (or create!) a meetup group to practice a foreign language.

The small players only show up in the good years, but the big dogs are *always* there.

So the networking opportunities are at their very best in the worst years. Don't hang out with the job hunters at the local or regional conference. Hang out with the job *givers* at the national conference. It's worth the money, I promise you.

One of my clients, a very important entity at a very large bank, has a saying: *follow the money.*

The money isn't in the boonies with the small fries; it's at the table with the big boys. The money isn't in coach; it's in business class.

More about that later.

CHAPTER SUMMARY

- It's not about what you do when layoffs are already happening; it's about what you did during all those months and years leading up to that time.

- If you have limited options, focus on the ones you have.

- Build your network and diversify your boss risk.

- Become indispensable at work.

- Take advantage of training and learning opportunities.

CHAPTER 6

HIDE

HIDING, THE SMART WAY
In Chapter 2, I told you that when the bull is staring you down, you can't run and you can't hide. You have to grab the bull by the horns — literally.

The same goes for a recession. You can't run forever from a recession, and you can't hide all the way, but you *can* run and you *can* hide in smaller ways. As long as you're doing it consciously, with a game plan in mind, and not just because you're scared, it can be an excellent move. That's what this chapter and the next chapter are about.

Let's start with hiding as a strategy. Remember: recessions don't last forever. As sure as they will come, they will also go. Things will get bad enough that the Fed will lower the interest rate and people will be tempted to borrow money and start businesses. The price of everything will get so cheap that some brave souls will stick their heads out of the bunker and decide that now's the time to build. People will get their cherry-pickers out of the closet, and see if the tree has grown some cherries. It might take a year for things to turn around, or it might take two, three, four, or five years, but it will happen. This is why hiding can be a good strategy. Hiding is all about setting yourself up somewhere relatively immune from a downturn, and then, when the economy picks up again, emerging from the shadows with even more experience and skills than before. Hiding can take two forms. The first is to go back to, or stay in, school. The second is to get yourself into a recession-proof industry. Let's look at the school option first.

HIDE IN SCHOOL
School is always an option. Whether it's a world-class university in another state, the community college around the corner, or an online degree program that you can access from your laptop while wearing your pajamas, there are options everywhere, for everyone, and for any budget.

The beauty of the hide-in-school option is that while you're hiding, you're also *building* — building skills that you can use when the economy recovers. Education is always part of your ongoing career development, but it can double as your full-time refuge when times are tough.

Because more and more education is moving online, going to school is easier now than it's ever been in the entire course of human history. In 2016, I finished a Master's in Negotiation, Conflict Resolution, and Peacebuilding that I did entirely online.

At the time I was living in Texas and the school was in California. Back in 2016, this was still somewhat of a novel idea. But today, who cares? Nowadays that's commonplace — especially after the COVID-19 pandemic shutdown.

Go back to school.

School is an easy option if you're young, single, and childless. No one is depending on you, so the loss of income for a few years is more manageable.

School is a tougher option if you're a mid-career professional with a family. If that describes you, you've got to have some serious savings that you're willing to burn through. Otherwise, you might need to have a spouse who can be the primary earner for awhile. Failing that, hiding out in school is probably a nonstarter for you as a way to recession-proof your life. Digging in, building, and investing are probably far better options for you.

School becomes an easier option again once you're an empty-nester. The kids are out of the house, you've got fewer people relying on you, and suddenly school is feasible. A lot of 50- and 60-somethings have a block when it comes to going back to school. It feels beneath them or embarrassing somehow. But school is not just for young people anymore. I know a guy who got a golden handshake from his company when he was in his 50s, and took the opportunity to go back to school all the way up to a PhD. My great-aunt — now of blessed memory — did her Bachelor's degree when she was 57, and a Master's degree when she was 61! She continued working until she was 84.

Going back to school when you're older is a great way to reinvent yourself, rebrand yourself, and show that, in terms of energy and ambition and drive, you're still young at heart.

As long as you have valuable skills, no one is going to care when you got them. Plus, online degree programs make it easy to go back to school without having to leave the house and neighborhood where you've put down roots.

I've got more good news if you're an older worker. A lot of companies have moved from pensions to defined contributions. This makes employees responsible for their own retirement, and that means that companies are less cautious about hiring older workers who might want to retire soon. These days, it's also very common to hire older workers on contracts. At Prestige Economics, I hire contract workers all the time.

A number of these folks have been in their 50s and 60s who are seasoned professionals, quit the 9-5 grind, and now make a good living by working remotely.

Back in 2015, *TIME Magazine* recently had an article about the things we have now that, in the future, we'll think are ridiculous.[1]

One of the things on the list is *offices*.

This has only become more apparent in recent years — especially in the wake of the COVID-19 pandemic and associated economic shutdown. In fact, I expect many people who have been forced to work from home will never go back to work in offices ever again.

DRILL #9: KNOWING WHAT WOULD WORK

List 5 different formal education programs *you could pursue* in the next 5 years to boost your earning power and job security?

1. _____

2. _____

3. _____

4. _____

5. _____

DRILL #10: KNOWING WHAT YOU WANT

List 5 different formal education programs *you want to pursue* in the next 5 years to boost your earning power and job security?

1. _____

2. _____

3. _____

4. _____

5. _____

Stay in school.

What if you're *already* in school? The trick is to graduate into a good economy, and if that means delaying graduation by a few years, by all means, do it. Let's say you're 22, you've just graduated from a four-year program, and things are tough. The job market's horrible, you're stuck waiting tables and so are your friends, even that one overachiever who double-majored in computer engineering and business. You know it's going to be a few years before anything better comes up, and by then you'll have "unemployment scarring" written all over you.

Is this you? Then go to grad school.

Lock yourself up in the ivory tower for a couple more years, then come out fresh as a daisy, with a sparkling new degree. When you re-enter the job market, instead of having a dusty Bachelor's degree and two years of bagging groceries on your resume, you've got a Bachelor's *and* a brand-spanking-new Master's degree.

If your graduate program is fully funded, you might even make more money being a student than you would working a menial job — all the while building your skills and sidestepping unemployment scarring. I received full funding to get a Master's in Applied Economics, because they needed someone who would be willing to go through and translate all the personal articles and scores of rolls of microfilm owned by a famous Austrian economist, who published some of his most important works from the 1920s to the 1940s.

Whatever they want from you, if it means getting paid to get a degree, you have nothing to lose. PhD programs are usually fully funded, and you almost always have the option of pulling the ripcord and leaving them early with just a Master's degree. That gives you some flexibility in terms of when you enter the job market, so you can time it just right.

Actually, if you're 22, recently graduated, and mopping floors because the economy stinks, you've already waited longer than you should have. The time to decide on the stay-in-school option was when you were 21 and starting your senior year of college. Most graduate programs have application deadlines in the fall or winter for the next year. If the economic omens are bad, that's when you want to apply for that Master's degree, and avoid even one year of menial labor and unemployment scarring.

DRILL #11: KNOWING WHAT WOULD WORK
List 5 different formal education programs *you could pursue to postpone your entry into the job market* and build valuable skills:

1. _____

2. _____

3. _____

4. _____

5. _____

DRILL #12: KNOWING WHAT YOU WANT

List 5 different formal education programs *you want to pursue to postpone your entry into the job market* that could boost your earning power and job security:

1. _____

2. _____

3. _____

4. _____

5. _____

Boost your education ROI

ROI stands for return on investment. It's how much you get back from what you put in. Education is an investment, so you need to think about ROI just as carefully as you would if you were investing in the stock market.

Let me tell you about the best ROI on education I ever got.

A while back, I trained to be a Certified Negotiation Expert. This was a $300 course that took two days. When I bought my house, I saved $25,000, *at least*, because of the negotiation skills I learned in that course. If a penny saved is a penny earned, then I earned more than $80 for every one dollar I spent on that course. That's an amazing ROI.

How can you get ROI like that? One way is to choose a degree that is expensive (high investment), but also so beneficial for your career (high return) that it more than makes up for the cost. Professionally-oriented Master's degrees are like this.

Think business, finance, accounting, nursing. If you get a degree in nursing, you're shelling out serious money, but also qualifying yourself for one of those undeniably necessary professions that a recession can't touch. When people are sick, they need a nurse, recession or not. If you're already in the nursing profession, you can go back to school to be a Physician's Assistant or a Nurse Practitioner, and boost your income significantly.

An MBA — a Master's of Business Administration — can also be one of those high investment, high return degrees. A top degree will probably cost you a couple hundred grand, but the returns are also huge. Consider doing your MBA in the city where you want to work. That way, you're getting all the knowledge *and* you're getting unparalleled access to the business network in that city. Your MBA will be worth many times the $100,000 to $200,000 or more that you're putting into it.

If you're a lawyer, you probably know by now that your profession was decimated in the last economic downturn. The law schools were cranking out JD's like sausages, and you ended up with negative ROI. Consider getting an LLM — a Master of Laws — to give you that edge over the competition. In your LLM, specialize in something like taxation. Law firms aren't always hiring, but accounting firms definitely are.

These are educational options with a high return. But, really, any degree is better than none. No matter what your profession, there's a way to catapult yourself with more education. A GED is infinitely better than nothing, an Associate's Degree is better than a GED, a Bachelor's degree is better than an Associate's Degree, and on and on.

Education is the great equalizer. It's as simple as that.

The more education you have, the less likely you are to be unemployed. And education correlates positively with higher incomes. It's a proven fact: the more education you have, the less likely you are to be unemployed and the more money you earn. In Figure 6-1, you can see these dynamics in U.S. data from 2019, before COVID-19 — when the job market was hot.

Figure 6-1: Unemployment and Earnings by Education[2]

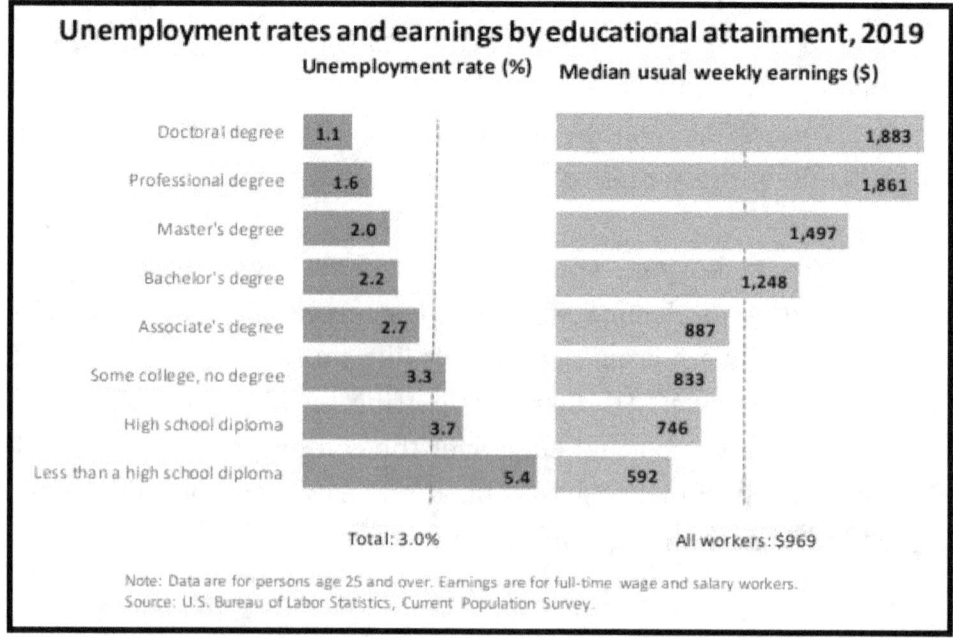

But these dynamics were also true after the onset of the COVID-19 pandemic and recession.

In May 2020, the unemployment for people with no high school diploma was at 19.9 percent, while it was 15.3 percent for those with a high school diploma, 13.3 percent for those with some college, 7.4 percent for Bachelor's degree holders, and only 5.6 percent for those with Master's degrees. This means that in May 2020, there was a 14.3 percentage point difference between the unemployment rate for people who didn't finish high school, compared to people who held Master's degrees.[3]

What a difference education makes in the job market!

And you should always be thinking about your ROI — your return on investment of pursuing education as well as any other professional strategy.

Another strategy for getting high educational ROI is to reduce your costs. The lower the cost (investment), the less benefit (return) you need to get from it, in order to make it worth it. For instance, if a university is offering you full funding to go to graduate school, you can be pretty blue-sky with your degree choice and still get good ROI. You can do that PhD in Sociology you always dreamt of, graduate debt-free and put "Dr." in front of your name. You probably won't be earning as much as an MBA graduate, but you also got that degree for free. What's there to lose? Conversely, if you're paying out of pocket, you need to be choosy. You may want to think twice about going deeply into debt to get that PhD in Medieval History.

To lower your costs, consider doing an online program. For that Master's in Negotiation, Conflict Resolution, and Peacebuilding that I completed in 2016, I've never once set foot in a physical classroom.

So the university can offer it for much less money.

Each course was around $900, and I needed to complete a dozen courses to earn the degree. That's not much more than $11,000 for an entire Master's degree.

It's hardly pocket change — but way less than a $200,000 MBA program.

There's a way to reduce your costs even further, almost to zero, but you have to be careful with it. Before I started my Master's in Negotiation, Conflict Resolution, and Peacebuilding, a friend of mine said, "Don't bother with it. Just buy the books and read them."

He was partly right: you can learn the skills just from reading the books, and that would hugely reduce your costs and boost your ROI. If you check the books out of a library, your monetary investment would be *zero*.

But here's the problem. You wouldn't get that piece of paper at the end that *proves* you read those books. Plus, what is the chance that, without the structure and deadlines of the degree, you'll *actually* read all those dozens of books?

If you're like me — a busy professional whose most precious and scarce resource is time — it really helps to have that external pressure to prioritize the coursework. Quizzes at the end of each reading assignment really force you to read and absorb every word. Group papers and projects force you to do the work and the reading.

It's kind of like going to gym. If you pay for a gym membership, you're going to want to get your money's worth, but you might not prioritize it without external pressure. If you have a group you work out with or a personal trainer, you now have a person or group of people to hold you accountable. If you didn't have that pressure of accountability, it would be easy to be lazy and put off the cardio forever.

That benevolent pressure is one of the values of taking a formal degree course rather than going all DIY on your education.

If structure is something you need — and there's really no shame in that — you're probably best off in a SMOC, which stands for *simultaneous massive online course*. When you take a SMOC, you have to log in at a certain time, turn in assignments according to deadlines, and so forth, just like in a "real" class in a bricks-and-mortar university. If you don't need that kind of structure to motivate yourself, or if you're super busy and need to do the course little by little over a long period of time, or if you've got tons of time on your hands and want to plow through the course quickly, don't do a SMOC. Do a traditional at-your-own-pace online course and complete it as quickly or as slowly as you like.

One more tip to boost your education ROI: Returns on investment are more than just monetary things; they're emotional, too. If you're stuck doing something that feels below you, like waiting tables with a Bachelor's degree, taking some online courses can really improve your self-esteem. That in itself has a return. As for the investment side of the coin, your costs aren't just the money you spend on the courses, but the blood, sweat, and tears required to do all the coursework. That really matters.

So, before you sign up for a class, look at the books that are on the reading list. If you like them, if they look interesting, then take the class. If they look boring and annoying, then you're going to hate the class. That raises your investment and lowers your ROI. Don't take the class.

Finally, think about how long you expect to benefit from the education you'll be getting. How long will it take to get a positive ROI from your education, and how many years will it keep bringing additional ROI to you? About halfway through the Master's in Negotiation, I almost doubled my money by implementing the new skills I learned in a negotiation. Imagine that: doubling your money before even finishing the degree.

Plus, I expect to continue my career for about 30 more years, and I'll be reaping the benefits of that degree the whole time. Think about that when examining education options. How long will it take for that Excel course or accounting course to pay off and have a positive ROI? Probably very quickly. How long will it continue to pay off? Probably for a long time.

HIDE IN A RECESSION-PROOF INDUSTRY

The other kind of hiding is to hang out in a recession-proof industry. A recession-proof industry is one that barely flinches, even when other industries are hurting bad. It is a safe haven in an economic maelstrom. The fancy word for a recession-proof industry is *acyclical*. That means that it doesn't go down with the rest of the economy. It keeps hiring even in the bad years.

You don't need to have a PhD in Economics to have a sense of which industries are recession-proof and which ones are recession- prone. It all comes down to human wants versus human needs. If people *need* it, they'll still pay for it, even when times are tough. If they only *want* it, they'll stop paying for it when times are tough. So need-based industries are recession-proof, while want-based industries are recession-prone.

Now ask yourself, what do people *need*? They need food. They need healthcare. They need education. They need protection from crime and foreign invasion, and they need someone to show up with a hose if their house goes up in flames. So grocery stores, hospitals, schools, and core government departments should do fine, recession or not.

Now ask yourself, what do people only *want*?

They want restaurant food. They want trendy new clothes and jewelry. They want luxury vacations. So tourism, hospitality, and retail boom in the good years, but bust in the bad years.

What about housing? Yes, people need shelter, but they don't need to have a *big* house, have a *new* house, or even own their home. In a recession, new household formation slows. People don't have income, so they delay moving out of their parents' basement, or they keep living with roommates, or they keep renting, or they stay in their current small house. Companies stop building new houses. So the housing and construction industries actually do very poorly in a recession.

In general, private-sector jobs are more recession-vulnerable than public-sector jobs. The government rarely lays people off. They might slow down the pace at which they hire people, they might cut the number of promotions they hand out, but they are very reluctant to get rid of anyone they've already hired. The government can raise debt in order to make up for short-term budget shortfalls. If the government downsizes, it will be slowly, with lots of sluggish bureaucracy, and it won't be because of a recession, it'll be because of long-term revenue concerns, or because of a major change in Congress or an executive mandate.

Right now, the U.S. military is in a recession of sorts. But even there, they're just slowing down their hiring, and letting the older employees slowly retire, rather than laying people off *en masse*.

At corporations, it's different. Profit is everything. The stock price falls on Wednesday and there might be layoffs on Thursday. At your private-sector job, you've probably been enjoying your yearly bonus. But remember, they call it a *bonus* for a reason — you might not get it. In a bad economic year, you almost certainly won't.

Any industry that is tied to demographics is recession-proof. The funeral industry is recession-proof, because people are always going to die. Healthcare is recession-proof, because people are always going to get sick. With baby boomers aging fast, and Obamacare expanding, these industries are actually growing. It's a great time to be an undertaker. It's morbid to say, but it's true.

Primary and secondary school education is similarly recession-proof. When a child turns five, he or she has to go to school, and needs to have a teacher. It's a law; it has nothing to do with the economy.

When property tax revenue drops, hiring slows down, but it can't grind to a halt because the kids need teachers and there are regulations dictating how many students you can have in a classroom. Add on top of that, the fact that grade school teachers are heavily unionized, and you've got yourself a recession-proof industry.

Higher education is less recession-proof, because unlike grade school, it's not mandatory and it's not free, and you can pack a lecture hall with 500 students if you want to.

For these and other reasons, university teaching is a tough gig these days, and rather vulnerable to economic downturns.

Unless you're one of the lucky few to get a permanent, "tenure-track" professor job, you'll be what they call an adjunct or sessional instructor, with low pay and no job security.

Accounting is recession-proof. Why? Because whether businesses are doing well or doing poorly, they need to keep track of just how well or poorly they're doing. If they're running a loss, all the more need for a bean-counter to add up all the tax write-offs.

Understanding the recession-vulnerability of your industry is one of the most important steps you can take to safeguard your economic future.

Take my father-in-law, for instance. He worked as a contractor in the construction business for many years. But that industry is *wildly* recession-prone. Surviving the bust years meant relocating, again and again. My father-in-law didn't want this. He wanted the luxury of staying in the same place, and who can blame him? So he retrained for a recession-proof industry, nursing. Eventually, he transitioned to be a procurement specialist — basically, a person who buys things — at a hospital.

This hospital is always going to need latex gloves, computers, stethoscopes, and whatnot, no matter how bad the economy gets. So he'll never be out of the job.

He's doesn't worry about the economy anymore, he doesn't need to travel, and he's as happy as a clam.

My father-in-law's story has a valuable lesson.

You might enter a recession-proof industry just as a temporary refuge, but don't be surprised if you end up staying there.

You might enjoy the stability of it, and the luxury to not have to pay attention to the business cycle.

Then you can throw this book away and just enjoy your life. On the other hand, if you like risk and excitement, making a killing in boom-and-bust industries like construction during the good years and then hiding out in stable industries during the bad years can make for a more varied and lucrative career.

It comes down to your personality and your priorities.

AFTER COVID-19
As in previous cycles, people make life-long career decisions based on traumatic experiences. And after the experience of the COVID-19 pandemic, people will most certainly be flocking to more roles in essential industries and in jobs where remote work is possible.

After all, people — especially young people — will have seen a big difference in the impact of the COVID-19 recession on tech workers versus non-essential service sector workers.

Overall workers are likely to be skeptical of non-essential and non-remote jobs for a long time to come. In fact, we could see the impact of the COVID-19 pandemic — and the associated pandemic economic shutdown — cast a multi-decade-long shadow on the careers of many people who want to make sure they have more options, rather than less.

CHAPTER SUMMARY

- Hiding is all about setting yourself up somewhere relatively immune from a downturn, and then, when the economy picks up again, emerging from the shadows with even more experience and skills than before.

- Hide in school, if you are young and unencumbered.

- Go back to school if your kids are out of the house.

- Look for a job in a recession-proof industry (e.g., government, healthcare, education, technology).

- COVID-19 is likely to incentivize people to seek out essential or remote working jobs, while avoiding non-essential service sector jobs for many years to come.

CHAPTER 7

RUN

RUN TO, NOT FROM

If the omens are bad, if your coworkers are starting to take their golden handshakes, if your city's Main Street is getting boarded up, you can cut and run. Running can take various forms: running to another place, running to another job title, running to another company, or running to another industry. You can also do two or three or even all four of these. Those double, triple, and quadruple runs are challenging, but sometimes possible; more about that later.

Running doesn't mean fleeing in terror. It doesn't mean giving up. Running is a carefully thought-out strategy. It's pulling up the stakes and moving your tent to a better campsite. If you're only thinking about what you're running *from*, you have the wrong attitude, and you're going to get yourself in trouble. You need to think just as much, or more, about what you're running *to*. Remember: the first rats off the sinking ship get the best deal. Those who stay will work longer and harder. By all means, jump ship, but have a plan for where you're going to scurry next.

People are innately averse to change. Leaving behind the city and the company (or even the *country* and the *industry*!) that you know so well is scary. It might not be fun. There will be challenges and sacrifices. But this is your livelihood that's on the line. You can't be lazy about it and you can't be ruled by fear.

If there are opportunities to escape the recession, if there is a professional oasis somewhere that could save you from burning through your savings and mortgaging your children's future, you need to think very seriously about going there.

I have a friend — he was one of my groomsmen — who discovered that there was limited upward mobility in the consulting firms that he was working for back during the recovery following the 2001 recession. You know what he did?

He moved to Dubai, in the United Arab Emirates. He'd never even been there before! But he did it, he made the move, and he has been very successful there.

You always need to have one eye open for opportunities like that.

Look back at your risk responses from Drill #6 in Chapter 4.

Is your region vulnerable? What about your industry? Is there another region or another industry where things are looking up?

You don't have to jump in headfirst. You can just dip your toe in. Looking at your options is always a no-regrets strategy.

SHOULD I RUN?

In a boom year, pay attention to the health of your *company* and your geographical *region*:

	Weak region	Strong region
Strong company	Think about running	Stay where you are
Weak company	Definitely run!	Think about running

In a bust year, pay attention to the health of your *company* and your *industry*:

	Weak industry	Strong industry
Strong company	Think about running	Stay where you are
Weak company	Definitely run!	Think about running

RUN TO ANOTHER PLACE

Moving physically to another city, state, or country is the scariest kind of running. It changes everything in your life: your job, your house, your neighbors, your circle of friends, your professional network, your spouse's career, your kids' friends and school, even your hobbies and your daily routines, and maybe even the language you use.

But when the choice is between staying in Detroit, Michigan or moving to Austin, Texas? You'd better move. If you're American, chances are that your ancestors came from somewhere else, looking for better economic opportunities. There are significant exceptions, of course. Native Americans were here far longer, although they may have crossed the land bridge for economic opportunity. And the ancestors of most African Americans were forcibly and tragically brought here as slaves.

But statistically speaking, if you're an American reading this book, you're probably the descendant of economic migrants. And if your ancestors could get up the gumption to leave all their relatives behind, cross an ocean, learn a new language, and build their way up from the bottom rung of a new country, you can hop in a car and get your tuchas to Texas.

If your ancestors did it, you can do it. I don't mean to get on a pulpit about this — I know that moving isn't easy and I know that not everyone can do it — but someone has got to bang this tin drum. No one is talking about this, and that is a shame, because moving can be your best bet to survive and thrive in an economic downturn.

America is a big country. Europeans like to make fun of Americans for not wanting to travel internationally, but they're forgetting just how big a country America is. The United States is almost two times the size of the entire European Union, which has 28 members and six candidate countries.

In the United States, you can move to hundreds of different micro-economies without ever leaving your country. This is a great and underappreciated advantage of being American. Most people in other countries don't have that advantage. You should make the most of it.

Where are the opportunities?

Let me tell you about some of the worst advice I've ever gotten. When I was finishing up my Master's in German and thinking of joining the workforce, I asked an academic advisor, a career academic, "Where do I find a job?"

He laughed and said, "Why are you asking me? I've never had a job!" Then he said, "Maybe the way that you get a job is you just move where you want to live, and then you start applying for jobs, and wait until you get one. I don't know." He was a good man and an excellent academic mentor, but he just didn't have the real-world answer that was going to help me pay the bills.

Lesson learned: don't expect much when you ask a university professor for advice about jobs. They might have been in the ivory tower too long, in cushy tenured jobs, and when it comes to real-world career stuff, they might not know how to survive.

The truth is, you can't just move where you want and then look for a job. You need to think about where the opportunities are, where the jobs are.

Remember from Chapter 2 that a recession isn't one giant, monolithic thing. It's a lot of little things.

Different places have different rhythms of growth, different economic vibes, and different things that drive their prosperity. In a recession, some places suffer a lot, some suffer a little, some don't suffer at all, and a few actually do really well.

And not every recession hits each region in the same way.

In the United States, the 2001 recession hit tech companies particularly hard, which was bad for Silicon Valley and places like Austin, Texas. And, of course, after September 11th, the New York economy suffered significantly in many ways.

This was different than after the Great Recession from 2007 to 2009, when the tech industry and both Silicon Valley and Austin were hit much less hard. The most negatively impacted places during and after that recession were places with some of the biggest housing bubbles — that burst. This included Las Vegas, Phoenix, Miami, parts of California, and a lot of other areas.

But following the Great Recession, the Midwest, on the other hand, was a lot stronger than the coasts. And the unemployment rates in the central United States were a lot stronger — with much more opportunity than the coastal states.

To see which places are busting and which are booming, the easiest thing to do is look at unemployment figures broken down by state. And like much of the other data and information I've shared, this is all free and available online.

Here's a link to Regional and State Unemployment Rates:
http://www.bls.gov/news.release/pdf/laus.pdf

When you look at the data, see if there is anything that surprises you. What you're really looking for are opportunities — and lower unemployment rates. Because even though there may be a recession. It doesn't hit all states evenly. Some places fair better than others, and if you know which states those are, you can know what options might make you more recession-proof.

After the recession ended in 2009, many people were surprised to see that out-of-the-way places like the Dakotas and Nebraska have been relative oases of prosperity in recent years, compared to places like California or New York.

And in May 2020, the unemployment rates ranged from a low of 5.2 percent in Nebraska to a high of 25.3 percent in Nevada. With food being a priority during the COVID-19 pandemic and people shying away from tourist destinations, the disparity isn't surprising.[1]

But the point isn't to understand why each state is different. It's that you need to know it's not enough to just guess where the jobs are, based on what places sound hot. You have to look at the data. And the data may surprise you.

Even better than looking at the state-by-state data is looking at the city-by-city data. After all, you wouldn't be moving to a whole state; you'd be considering moving to one part of a state, and that's what matters most. When looking at unemployment rates, the data for cities are grouped into broader urban regions known as MSAs — or Metropolitan Statistical Areas.

In May 2020, when the COVID-19 pandemic shutdown was just coming off the peak levels, the unseasonally adjusted average unemployment rate in the United States was a high 13.0 percent.

But unemployment rates for MSAs varied widely from a low of 4.8 percent in Logan, Utah and neighboring Idaho to 33.4 percent in Kahului-Wailuku-Lahaina, Hawaii.[2] Clearly, if you wanted to be somewhere recession-proof, you had options.

After all a 4.8 percent unemployment rate is quite low. But you would have needed to know where to look. Otherwise, you might have moved to Hawaii thinking it was cool, only to find more than one in three people were unemployed.

Here's a link to Metropolitan Statistical Area Unemployment Rates: http://www.bls.gov/news.release/pdf/metro.pdf

Looking abroad.

If you're prepared to make an international jump, look at the country-by-country data. Here's a link to Country Unemployment Rates from the World Bank: http://data.worldbank.org/indicator/SL.UEM.TOTL.ZS

If you work at a multinational company, a good way to run is to transfer to an overseas branch. Just because your company is laying off people in San Francisco doesn't mean they're not hiring like crazy in Dubai or Denmark.

Your company will likely pay to move your entire family. They may give you a living allowance. They may pay for your kids to attend an English-speaking international school. There are all kinds of perks.

Look at where your colleagues are transferring. Are people jumping from your local branch to the London branch? Is no one making the opposite jump? Look at your company's internal job board. If the London office is hiring, but your office is *not*, your office may be going down the tubes, while the London office is rocking. Think about making that move. Don't be the last one, when there are far more limited options.

There are a few special tricks if you want to move overseas. If you're hoping to transfer to an overseas branch of your company, start learning the language of one of the other countries your company operates in.

If your company is based in Japan, learn Japanese.

If it does a lot of business in Mexico, learn Spanish. Find multinational networking opportunities. You want to be schmoozing at international conferences, not just national and regional ones.

Other than that, do all the usual job-hunting things, which may seem obvious but are so often ignored. Things like: keep your resume updated and ready to send. Sign up for LinkedIn. Get on Indeed.com. For high-profile gigs, there's also TheLadders.com.

And keep learning.

You may have heard the saying: "Dress for a job you want, not the job you have." Well, I would say: learn skills for the job you want, not the job you have.

Remember that a human resources manager isn't going to look at your resume for five to 10 minutes. They're going to look at your resume for six *seconds*. At least that was the finding of a study by TheLadders.com called "Keeping an eye on recruiter behavior," which tracked recruiters' eye movements as they reviewed resumes. Actually, nowadays it's often less than six seconds, because the first filter of resumes will be done by a robot. Instead of getting six seconds, you're getting six milliseconds. That's why it's vitally important to have the right keywords on your resume, so you get through that first, utterly pitiless filter.

Where am I willing to live?

Be open to moving, but also respect your limits. Do this chapter's drills to start thinking about where you're willing to move and where you're not. Some readers are going to circle the whole globe. Other readers are going to make a teeny tiny dot right on their hometown. That's okay.

For instance, if someone in your family has a disability and your house is customized to accommodate it, you might not even be willing to move down the street. It all depends on your situation, your needs, and your personality.

Headhunters often try to suss out who in the family makes the decisions, who gets a vote. If you're single and childless, there's just one vote — yours — so your ability to move is endless. If you have a spouse, live-in parents, and so forth, there might be several people with veto power, and your options are more limited.

DRILL #13: THINK BIG!

HIGHLIGHT ON THE MAP BELOW WHERE YOU WOULD BE WILLING TO MOVE IN THE UNITED STATES[3]

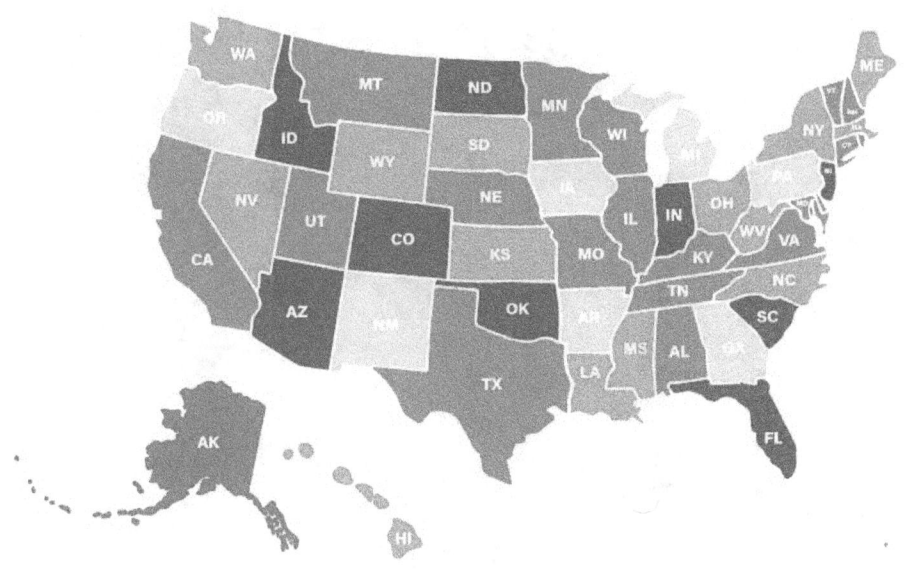

The ability and willingness to move will come down to your particular personal and family situation.

Before you narrow down your options, try and expand your thinking and the options you have. After you open the aperture and think big, you'll actually have a sharpened perspective on what the most reasonable and best options could be.

Just don't rule out the possibility of moving before you've looked hard at all the benefits it could give you — and the other members of your household with voting or veto powers.

DRILL #14: NOW, THINK EVEN BIGGER!

HIGHLIGHT ON THE MAP BELOW WHERE YOU WOULD BE WILLING TO MOVE IN THE WORLD[4]

RUN TO ANOTHER JOB, COMPANY, OR INDUSTRY

The other kind of running isn't physical — it's professional. If you're in a dying industry, a dinosaur profession, or a failing company, running from these things can actually be a more radical move than running from your region. On the upside, it means that you could bail from a losing proposition without changing your city, your house, or any other part of your life.

That can be a real win-win.

Where should I run to?

First, ask yourself: is it my industry that's hurting, or just my company, or just my particular *job* within that company and that industry?

If you're in autos and autos are rocking, but they're replacing factory workers with robots, your industry is fine. It's your job title that's endangered. Look for a different job in the same industry. If you're a cab driver and you're losing business to Uber, your industry — personal transportation — is fine, but your taxi company is in trouble. You might want to consider driving city buses.

If you're an accountant for a luxury hotel chain, and a recession is hitting your company hard, it's your industry that's the problem. It's highly recession-prone. Stay in accounting, but switch to a more stable industry, like food.

Be an accountant for a supermarket chain.

The data on which companies, industries, and job titles are doing well and which ones are doing poorly is available at the click of a mouse, for free. For companies, stock prices are the most obvious index of who's up and who's down.

You also have insider knowledge of your own company's outlook. Of course, you can't use that knowledge to buy or sell stock — that's illegal — but nothing is stopping you from using that knowledge to decide whether to stay aboard or jump ship! That's not insider trading.

It's just smart living.

As for the outlook for specific industries and jobs, the U.S. government keeps close track of what's hot and what's not. The U.S. Bureau of Labor Statistics maintains historical data for — and predictions of — job growth by sector.

The information is freely available online at:
http://www.bls.gov/emp/ep_table_104.htm

How do I run?

When it comes to switching careers, there's good and bad news. The bad news is that HR managers are generally looking for *proven hires*. They want to fill a vacancy with someone who has already succeeded in *exactly* that job in *exactly* that industry. That's unfortunate for someone who is looking to make a career change.

You get caught in a catch-22: "They want to hire someone with five years of industry experience. But how can I get five years of industry experience, if no one in that industry will hire me?!?"

Good news: there's a trick to lowering this hurdle. It's an idea that was first put forth in *What Color Is Your Parachute?*

It takes a little bit of explaining, but it is important to understand.

Let's keep things simple, and think about just two things: your job title, and your industry. It's virtually impossible to change both at once.

But it's not that hard to change your job title while staying in your same industry. It's also not that hard to change your industry while keeping your job title.

So, if you want to switch your industry *and* your job title — which is an excellent move if you're trapped in a really hopeless part of the economy — you just need to make *one* of those moves at a time. Switch job titles, then switch industries — or switch industries, then switch job titles. It's a pivot approach.

What do you do?

Just make one move at a time. Do the pivot.

Let's consider some challenges from the recent past.

For instance, let's say that you were working as a cashier at Blockbuster before it went bust. You saw the four horsemen of the Apocalypse; you knew you needed to run. You always wanted to manage a grocery store.

But no one is willing to hire you into that role. After all, you don't have experience as a manager, and you don't have experience at a grocery store. Hiring you would be a huge risk.

Well, you could have worked your way up from cashier to manager at Blockbuster, then make the jump from video store manager to grocery store manager. Alternately, you could make the jump from video store cashier to grocery store cashier, then work your way up to grocery store manager. Either might have worked, but it would have likely taken two steps.

Similarly, if you were working on an oil rig in California when oil prices collapsed in 2015 and early 2016, you might have wanted to run. Low oil prices and industry warnings from the Fed and others indicated oil and gas was an industry in recession. Plus, California was a region that had been unusually sluggish to recover from the Great Recession. So, to made the pivot, you would have needed to change region and industry.

The good news for oil and gas is that some parts of the business — like pipelines in the Midwest and the Gulf Coast — will continue to operate even when the economy slows and prices collapse. And sometimes, pipeline throughput — the amount of oil and gas going through the pipes — actually increases with lower prices, because lower prices incentivize more demand.

And of course, sometimes there's a need to do a triple pivot.

During and after the Great Recession, Detroit was one of the hardest hit metros economically. And manufacturing suffered as well. So, if you had been a floor worker at a factory in Detroit in the late 2000s, you would have been in an endangered profession, endangered industry, and endangered region.

To do a triple pivot, you would have needed to cross-train your way into being a floor manager (change of job title). Then transfer to another facility (change of region). Then switch to managing a call center (change of industries). It might take many years, but you would have been better off than if you'd let the invisible hand of the economy bat you around like a tether ball.

RUNNING WITH THE BULL MARKETS
I've moved over 20 times since I was 18, so my story is as good as any another to illustrate all the reasons you might want to run and all the benefits it can give you. I call it Running with the Bull Markets. Focusing on the positive — a bull market is one where everyone is buying — is the key to that "running to" (rather than "running from") mentality I mentioned before.

After I completed my Master's of Applied Economics, I was hired by the Chief Economist at Wachovia in Charlotte, where I worked in the corporate and investment banks. In late 2007, I was working there when the risks of a global banking crisis were becoming obvious. I could tell that things were not going to end well for banking. I could see that a big recession was coming.

You see, at the time, banks were selling asset-backed securities and mortgage-backed securities in bundles and tranches.

They were taking mortgages, slicing and dicing them, and selling them in a way that almost no one understood. The way I like to describe these financial packages is that they were wedding cakes made of dog crap.

They looked pretty, as long as you didn't take a bite and find out what was inside. The ingredients were: a small bowl of the world's finest sugar (AAA rated mortgages), a bigger bag of some moderately okay flour (BBB rated mortgages), and a giant pile of dog crap (junk bond mortgages).

Well, in August of 2007, a fund manager in Europe took a bite of one of these crap cakes and found out what was inside. He raised the alarm.

Within days, the Fed and the European Central Bank were injecting hundreds of billions of dollars into the global economy to keep things afloat.

That's a desperate measure reserved for desperate times, and it was caused by major players in the markets getting spooked and cashing out. Any investor worth his salt saw this for what it was: red alert. It was sell, sell, sell. I remember going into a Monday meeting of the corporate risk committee, which included the Chief Risk Officer, and everyone was just freaking out. These were risk executives at one of the largest banks in the United States, and they were *scared.*

The next day I had a meeting with my team, my boss, my boss's boss, and my boss's boss's boss. Even my boss's boss's boss was scared. He was as pale as a ghost, and I knew it was time to seriously consider getting out. I couldn't trade stock around all this insider knowledge, but I could definitely trade my career around it. I decided to run.

Where to run?

Luckily, a friend of mine from graduate school had been working in Germany at McKinsey and Company, a top-ranked consulting firm. He and his colleagues had been trying to recruit me, and they were on my list of the five to 10 people who would hire me in a pinch.

This was the pinch.

After the meeting on Tuesday with my boss's boss's boss, I called up my friend and got a job interview that Friday in Cologne, Germany. I was on a plane to Europe the very next day.

I got the job.

The negotiation was minimal, because I needed to get out so I didn't have much bargaining power. I put everything I owned on earth onto a boat headed for Germany. From the interview to my first day on the job — and living on another continent — took just one month, which is pretty crazy.

The running *from* was pretty compelling: a publicly owned company that was going to tank when shareholders got spooked. The running *to* was equally important: a privately owned company whose owners would stay in for the long haul.

On top of that, I had a Master's in German, I had done German television interviews with Bloomberg Germany TV, and I had met plenty of times with German executives on behalf of Wachovia. I knew what I was getting into.

Running from recession again.

I settled into my job at McKinsey in Germany and patted myself on the back. I was safe now. I had insulated myself from the crap cake backlash. Or had I? I was in the Risk Practice wing of McKinsey, and in the spring of 2008, we had an offsite meeting outside of Frankfurt at Castle Falkenstein (yes, it's a real place).

It was at that meeting that I got some shocking information: the biggest buyers of those mortgage-backed securities were the German banks. They had bought the crap cakes. The tsunami had reached German shores. It was time to run again.

Within days of that meeting at Castle Falkenstein, I quietly asked to transfer back to the United States. McKinsey's New York office has stopped accepting transfers, which was a very bad sign.

But the office in Houston was still accepting. It made sense: Houston is America's oil capital, and oil prices were rising to record highs at that time. The choice was clear.

I requested a transfer to McKinsey's office in Houston, and got it. I put everything I owned on earth onto a boat headed back for the United States. That was the second time I crossed the Atlantic Ocean running from the same thing: recession. I was also running toward opportunity — and I found it in Texas.

The great escape.

No rest for the wicked. Pretty soon after I arrived in Houston, the U.S. recession was in full swing. Even oil prices were hurting. McKinsey's Houston office started to feel the crunch. Bonuses and promotions were drying up, and most of my colleagues were working 16 hours a day without a single billable hour. That's a bad sign. It was time to run again. I requested and received a very nice VSP.

That's when I started Prestige Economics. I could operate that business from anywhere, so there was no one obvious place to run to. I had unlimited choice of geography. So I went through a filter process, which is something I recommend for anyone starting a new business.

The first part of the filter process was asking myself where my network was. The answer was Moscow, Frankfurt, London, New York, Charlotte, and Houston. I decided I wanted to live in the United States, so that narrowed the list down to just three options: New York, Charlotte, and Houston. I wanted to live somewhere warm, so that knocked New York off the list. I wanted to live somewhere economically healthy, which knocked Charlotte off the list.

Once I had quit McKinsey, I realized that there was nothing tying me to Houston.

Austin is close to Houston, and costs were lower in Austin, so I could live better there for less. Houston's economy hinges on oil prices, which is boom-and-bust, while Austin depends on the state government, a big healthcare sector, and a large public university, all of which are much more recession-proof industries.

So I made the run to Austin and its stable economy.

I'm happy here in Austin, but you never know.

I may move again — and so might you.

CHAPTER SUMMARY

- Running can take various forms: running to another place, running to another job title, running to another company, or running to another industry.

- Focus on what you're running *to,* not what you're running *from.*

- Unemployment varies widely by region, industry, and profession, so do all of the research before packing up and heading out.

- The more open you are to change, the more options you have.

CHAPTER 8

BUILD

IF YOU BUILD IT...

When recessions come, options disappear. When you build something, options reappear. If you build smart and build right, you won't need to dig in to your current job, because you'll have other options.

You won't need to hide in school, because you'll be making money even in the bad years. You won't need to run, because you can make a go of it right here, right now.

You can build yourself, or you can build something outside of yourself — a business. Let's take each of these in turn.

BUILD YOURSELF

Building yourself means building your skills, your credentials, and your network. It's about growing You, Inc. into new markets. It's about expanding your brand. By doing this, you keep your options open. You reduce the chance of unemployment.

You also reduce the *length* of unemployment — which will minimize employment scarring and its terrible effects on long-term earnings. Remember my father-in-law: he went from contractor to nurse to hospital purchasing manager. It was a career *run*, but made possible only through *building*.

Education does not end with high school or college. It is lifelong. When I worked in banking, it might as well have been a law: if you want a promotion, first you needed to get another degree, another certificate, or another professional designation. It's equally true if you're in medicine, finance, trading, corporate strategy, or IT.

Don't be a couch potato

Let me be blunt. No one is going to hold it against you if you've been out of the job for a few months or even a few years. What they *will* hold against you is if you've spent that whole time sitting on your couch eating Cheetos and watching reruns of *Seinfeld*.

They *should* hold it against you — because there were so many ways to build yourself during that time. Watching sitcoms was not one of them.

At one point, Prestige Economics did a couple of executive search projects. We helped big companies find world-class executive talent.

Even with these high-performing candidates, you sometimes see a guy who lost his job three years ago and has giant hole on his resume. He did bupkis for three whole years. Is that someone you'd want to hire? Nope. You want to hire someone with hustle, drive, energy, hunger.

If a hiring manager sees that you've been unemployed for awhile, they won't throw your resume into the circular file. But they will ask you, "What did you do during that time to improve yourself?"

When that question comes, you need a rock-solid answer. No matter how small, list it on your resume: the online course, the language you've been dabbling in.

I have a friend who finally went back to school after 15 years to do an executive MBA. It's never too late.

Build yourself cheaply

You can read Chapter 5 for lots of ideas on how to build your skills without spending a lot of money out of pocket. I'll just say a few words here.

Get your company to pay for your training during the good years. That's when they have the budget. No matter how good the good years are, a recession is going to come sooner or later, so don't wait.

Take advantage of that free training while you can.

Volunteer. It's no cost to you and it has a positive impact on your community. Plus, because you're not getting paid, organizations will let you get experience at all kinds of jobs that you would never be hired to do. Are you trying to make the jump to finance? Ask that soup kitchen if they'd like some help with their budget estimates. Why would they say no? Would you like to expand your marketing skillset? Ask that animal shelter if they'd let you help them with their fliers and their Facebook page.

It's amazing what nonprofit organizations will let you do, even when you have no experience. You can serve on their board of directors. Imagine that. It looks great on a resume and it's available to anyone who shows interest in the organization. I became a volunteer dog trainer at the Houston SPCA. I didn't get a job out of this, but I gained some valuable "soft" skills. Patience is probably the most important one.

Volunteering is a great way to make that double pivot that I talked about in Chapter 7. You're stuck in that catch-22: you want the job, but they won't hire you unless you've already done it. Solution: volunteer for that kind of job at a nonprofit, and then you can show an employer that you've already done the job you want.

In my current role as the VP of Finance at The Texas Lyceum, I built an investment committee, created investment policies, formed an audit committee, and started the process of doing an audit of the organization. These have all been tremendous opportunities to build and demonstrate finance skills that I might not have otherwise been as easily given in a for-profit entity.

Stand out in the crowd.

Part of building skills is being out there and being *visible*. This is especially important during a recession, because during a recession, lots of people are looking for work and hiring managers just get carpet-bombed with resumes.

Sure, they've got the pick of the litter, but it doesn't make their lives easier. It just means more resumes to dig through.

Plus, during a recession, companies like to cut their HR departments, because they're not hiring as many new people. So you've got half as many HR people wading through twice as many job applications, and they get grumpy and overworked and sloppy. They might even cut their usual six seconds per resume down to three seconds, just to get through them all.
Recessions are exhausting times for HR people. So how do you get a job under these conditions?

Don't think of the HR people as gatekeepers or adversaries. Think of them as what they are: people just like you. They've got a tedious and thankless job, sifting through hundreds of resumes searching for that one gem.

Don't hate them for not noticing yours.

Instead, help them out. Make it obvious that your resume is the one they want to pick. A great way to do that is to keep training, keep learning, and cram your resume full of those keywords and credentials that they're looking for.

Also, don't be afraid to call a headhunter.

I'm talking about the connecting-applicants-with-jobs kind of headhunter, not the collecting-resumes-for-no-reason kind of headhunter. Call the first type. Don't call the second type.

What a headhunter does is fill the gap between job seekers and the people who want to hire them. It's not much different from a book agent or any other kind of service-based middleman. A good headhunter will get your resume into the right hands — and lots and lots of them. The more people who have your resume, the better.

Network like crazy.

A huge part of building yourself is building your network. I know it's a cliché. I know you've heard it a thousand times. But it's so fundamental, and so often ignored, that I have to mention it, over and over.

If you're still reading this book rather than putting it down and making some calls and sending some emails and signing up for some conferences, then I haven't mentioned it enough times yet. Get thee to an industry conference. Find the big dogs. Network, network, network.

You need that list of five to 10 people you can call any time that would give you a job. Whatever your career — blue collar, white collar, IT, cosmetics, anything — you need that list. *You need that list.*

I'm talking about five to 10 people you could call right now that would give you a job *tomorrow*. I'm talking about five to 10 deep, meaningful business relationships that you could leverage if things got bad.

That might sound hard, but remember that those five to 10 people don't need to be CEOs or anything, and the jobs don't need to be your dream job. One of those people could be your cousin Tony who's got a convenience store that you could go work at if things get really rough. That's fine. One of those people could be your mom who has an accounting office and would hire you for some part-time clerical work.

That's a job. That counts.

If you don't have that list of five to 10 people, you need to put this book down and go to some conferences, go to some dinner parties, network like your career depends on it — because it does.

When you're in school, you're usually completely disconnected from that list. The only people you're meeting are other students, who don't have full-time jobs, and professors, who sought refuge in the ivory tower, which is remarkably insulated from the rest of the world.

When you get out of school, you might have no names at all on your list. This makes getting a job a big challenge for a new graduate. On-campus recruiting is a good way to get around this.

Make sure to sign up for as many on-campus recruiting events as possible. Then, try to lock in a job offer before you graduate, to hedge your career prospects — and future earnings trajectory — against the risk of recession.

If you're a young professional, new in your career, maybe you have just two or three people on your list. That's when headhunters become important — their job is to add people to your list.

Doing a continuing education program, or a company-funded training program, is another good way to meet people with jobs. Really, that's who you want to meet: people with jobs. People without jobs might be great friends, but they're not great business associates.

Keep in mind, though, that the best time to network is not during a recession.

The best time to network is during the good years.

Then, when the downturn comes, they can help you.

You can also help *them*: it's not just a self-serving thing. If you network during a recession, you're going to meet a lot of people like you, people who are pumping you for a job — or who are being pumped for a job.

Let me tell you a story about how networking really helped me during my career — and how I had to push to make it happen.

When I was working at Wachovia in Charlotte, I asked my boss if the company would pay for me to attend OPEC meetings, where all the big names in the oil industry go.

He sent me once, but after that, he didn't think it was worth my time.

I went anyway. I asked for time off, and used it to go to the conference, and paid for it myself. I invested in my own career. So there I was, literally at a palace having dinner with the Saudis and the Kuwaitis and all of the other OPEC ministerial groups and delegations.

This was the real deal.

I was in Vienna at Schönbrunn, the second biggest palace in Europe, and dudes dressed like Mozart were serving us dinner. At one end of the hallway the Kuwaiti National Philharmonic was playing, and at the other end the Vienna Symphony was playing.

At the end of dinner, the dudes dressed like Mozart gave us the goody bags for the party, which were small black leather boxes. When I opened my box, I gasped. Inside the boxes were solid gold coins commemorating the event. Solid. Gold. Coins.

Now, that's a party. And that's the place to network.

But how much did I pay for it? Hardly anything. I used frequent flyer miles to get there, and I stayed at an inexpensive hotel.

At the time, I had a colleague, an energy analyst, who criticized me greatly for using my own money and time to go to this conference.

But you know what that guy was doing?

He was finishing up an MBA, spending probably a couple hundred grand to go hang out with a bunch of guys in their late 20s who, maybe, 10 years in the future, *might* become big shots.

Meanwhile, I was spending just a thousand bucks to hang out with royalty, oil ministers from foreign countries, and energy analysts from leading oil companies. I was in the orangery of a palace — the place where they grew oranges in the winter for the Empress — while being served dinner by dudes dressed like Mozart who gave me a solid gold coin as a party favor.

So think about that before you go and spend $200,000 to do that top-level MBA. Is there another, much cheaper investment that you could be making right now to build your network?

Even the cost of taking the GMAT — the entrance exam for an MBA — and paying the application fee for half a dozen schools might be more than what it costs to go to an industry conference.

Look, I'm a big fan of formal education, and MBAs and other professional degrees have solid ROIs, but they are not the only game in town. Be wary of the one-size-fits-all recipe for professional advancement.

Besides, the real goal of the MBA is to jumpstart your network, and there may be other, faster, cheaper ways to do that right now.

Are you in finance?

Then go to the AFP, the Association of Financial Professionals. You'll meet treasurers, CFOs, and top accountants.

If you're in the global metals business, you need to go to London Metals Exchange Week, or LME Week. Whatever your field, there's a conference out there just like that. Go to the national and international conferences, where the big players show up. Meet them, talk to them, and stand out in a good way.

If your company won't pay for you to go to conferences where the big players are, go anyway. One or two thousand dollars is a small price of admission to hang out with the big dogs. It's a tiny fraction of what you would spend on an MBA. Just one word of caution: don't make it too obvious to your boss that you're going to the conference in the hopes of getting a better job. Emphasize to your boss the *skills* and *knowledge* that you're building, and how they will benefit your boss and team in your day-to-day role.

The most powerful piece of advice in this book.

I'm about to spill my biggest secret. This is a career-building trick that is so powerful and so little-known that I'm legitimately torn about whether or not to include it in this book. I don't know if I want to give it away. But I will.

Here's the secret: *fly business class.*

If you learn one thing from this book — aside from having five to 10 solid job contacts on speed dial — this should be it: *fly business class!*

I know, I know, it sounds crazy. Who's got the money to fly business class? You're just trying to survive! But I'm telling you, flying business class offers *the* best ROI for any networking you're ever going to do.

These days, I'm not flying much. But prior to the COVID-19 pandemic, I would only fly business class. And it wasn't just because it's more comfortable. (I'm 6 foot 3.) It's because that's where the big players sit. Who do you meet in business class?

You meet people with the budget to fly in business class. If they have the budget to fly in business class, then guess what? They probably have the budget to hire you. They probably have a great network, a great job, a lot of power, or all three. These are often C-level executives — CEOs, COOs, CFOs, etc.

Are you flying to L.A.? You'll probably be sitting next to an executive in the entertainment or music business.

Are you flying to Houston? You'll probably be sitting next to a petroleum boss. You also meet a lot of successful salespeople, making the fly-business-class trick especially good for anyone who wants to work in sales.

Sure, it's a crapshoot. You might end up sitting next to someone who doesn't speak English, or you might end up sitting next to the spouse or parent or child of a big shot. But this is the exception. Your odds are very good. I've been doing this for awhile now, and I would estimate that 75-80 percent of the time you sit in business class, you're sitting next to a very serious businessperson. Your odds are even better if you fly on a weekday in or out of a city where there's some action.

Sure, you might meet these same people at a conference, but you also might not. The top people are often in meetings the whole time. Sitting on a plane is one of the only times that they're not on the phone, in meetings, or being mobbed by various people who want their time.

It's one of the only times where no one can get to them — except you. You have one, two, or three uninterrupted hours for a one-on-one meeting. That's a very, very rare opportunity — and it can yield a very high ROI.

And another benefit: the people in business class aren't thinking, "I'm sitting next to someone who is unemployed and hunting for a job." They're thinking, "I'm sitting next to someone who can afford business class. I'm sitting next to someone who is in demand." They'll want you much more if they think that other people want you, too.

Flying business class projects success, even when you're down on your luck. And flying business class to get a job is guerilla job hunting — they'll never expect to see you prospecting!

It's like dressing for the job you want. Sit where the job you want is. I have many clients that I met at the front of the plane. If I ever find myself unemployed, I would fly first class and I bet after just a few flights, I'd have a job offer. If you're still thinking, "But it's so expensive!" think about it this way.

Everyone who can possibly afford it needs to set aside some money each year for building themselves and their network, even if it means dipping into savings. For example, at McKinsey, the number often cites internally was that the Firm spent around $25,000 per year on each employee for continuing education. That's how important it is.

Let's say that one year you set aside just $1,000, and let's say you're already traveling frequently for your job. If it costs you $100 per flight to upgrade to business class, then your $1,000 budget buys you 10 whole chances to make an important business connection. On seven of those flights, you meet a big dog. Three of those are in industries you're interested in. And one of them offers you a job. For the price of traveling to visit just one client, or attending just one conference, you got yourself a job. It's a lot more pleasant than fishing for business cards in Fuddruckers fishbowls. And if you're already flying for other reasons, paying for that upgrade is affordable and it is money very, very well spent.

If you've already shelled out $500 to fly to a national industry conference, spend another $100 to upgrade and you're likely to sit next to one of the most important people who is also attending that conference.

With that kind of top-notch interaction, your conference networking will be off to a great start.

To maximize your ROI, short-haul domestic flights are usually your best bet. On long-haul international flights, upgrading costs much more without much more benefit. You're only sitting next to one person, so you can network just as much in one hour as you can in eight. Also, don't fly on Monday mornings or Friday nights.

People are often too tired to talk then, and they may just want to nap. Plus, the most series executives have the income and authority to set their own schedules, which means they plan their travel for minimum family disruption. Translation: they don't usually fly early Monday or late Friday.

The middle of the day in the middle of the week is when executives tend to fly. Also, keep in mind that if you're flying with your family, upgrading is even more expensive, and pretty useless for networking — you'll spend the whole flight networking with your spouse, and that doesn't get you anywhere.

Of course, buying that seat next to the big player is just the first step. The second part is salesmanship. You're a salesperson now. What are you selling? You're selling you.

You've plopped down $100 to be there, you've got an hour or two, and the clock's ticking. You can't just sit there enjoying the free drinks and playing Angry Birds on your phone.

You've got to make the most of it. Be interesting, and be interested. The conversation starter I always use is, "So, are you heading home or heading away?" Then roll in from there.

This is one of the secrets to my success. I always sit in the front — and I hope to see you there!

BUILD A BUSINESS
The other building you can do in an economic downturn is building a business. There are lots of good reasons to start a business. It's an opportunity to create eulogy lines, not just resume lines.

A business becomes part of who you are, and not just something you do. Even if it fails, it's something you'll talk about and remember your whole life. You'll have become a more insightful business person, a more seasoned professional. It forces you to get better at many different things. Unless you invest money you don't have and end up losing your house, you'll come out of a business venture smarter, savvier, and stronger than before.

When I started my business, I probably had five people on the list of people I could call for a job. Now I have at least 50, thanks to my business.

Starting a business also means finally being paid what you're worth, because let's face it: the only person who will pay you what you're worth is you. Everyone else will pay you less — because otherwise they wouldn't be making a profit off of you.

If your company is paying you $50,000 a year, you're probably worth many times that. You get your $50,000, and your company gets the rest of the $500,000 of business that you bring in. Karl Marx called this process alienation. The only way to avoid it is to own your own business. Everything you produce, you keep.

Some people will tell you that the great thing about owning your own business is that you don't have a boss. That's a ridiculous notion. You will always have a boss. Everyone has a boss. If you own a business, your bosses are your customers or clients, and they can fire you just like a regular boss can. But when you have your own business, at least you've got *many* bosses. If one fires you, you've got others to fall back on. You're diversifying your boss risk. You're in a much better bargaining position, because you've got multiple offers. Remember: *whoever has options has power*. That is a great benefit to owning a business.

Start your business during a recession.

Believe it or not, a recession can be the best time to start a business. Many successful companies were founded in a trough: GE, IBM, GM, Disney, Tollhouse Cookies, Burger King, Microsoft, CNN, and Apple, to name just a few. Very few people want to build a business when the economy is rocking and bonuses are at record levels.

I started my business in my kitchen in 2009. The economy was still recovering from the Great Recession. I knew that bonuses would be low, so this was a good time to start. Since then, we've been ranked #1 in forecasting in 25 different categories.

DRILL #15: STARTING A BUSINESSES

List 5 to 10 businesses you'd like to start.

1. _____

2. _____

3. _____

4. _____

5. _____

6. _____

7. _____

8. _____

9. _____

10. _____

Remember from Chapter 4 the idea of *opportunity cost*. In a nutshell, it means: what you give up to get something else. If you date Susie, you can't date Annie. If you have a pet mouse, you can't have a pet cat. If you start a serious business, you can't hold down a full-time job.

When the economy is bad, your opportunity costs for starting a business are low. If you're out of work, you're not sacrificing a job in order to start a business. If your job stinks because all your colleagues left and you got stuck with their workload, you're not sacrificing much if you quit that job and start a business. At McKinsey, when things were getting tough, I knew consultants who were working 16 hours a day on client development projects, but they were bringing in zero billable hours. What are you giving up by leaving that? Nothing.

Figure 8-1: Businesses Started During a Recession[1]

Top Companies Formed During a Recession	
Company	Year Founded
General Electric	1890
IBM	1896
General Motors	1908
Disney	1923
Tollhouse Cookies	1933
Burger King	1953
Microsoft	1975
CNN	1980
Apple	1975/2001

On top of that, if starting your business means hiring staff, during a recession there are going to be lots of qualified people looking for work and they will be willing to work for less. Starting a business in a recession is buying low, which is the first rule of investing.

You'll be competing with firms who are shrinking and laying people off. Meanwhile you're hiring, you're growing, you're brand-new and shiny, and that looks very good to potential clients.

Find your unique value proposition.

To start a successful business, first you need to figure out what your *value proposition* is. "Value proposition" is consultant-speak for "what you bring to the table." It's the thing that makes you special, the thing that you provide to your customers that they can't get elsewhere.

If you're starting a business, congratulations, you are now an entrepreneur.

Entrepreneur is a French word that is made of *entre*, which means "between," and *preneur*, which means "one who takes."

You are taking your clients between one thing and another. That's your key to success. Find the gap that your customer can't cross. It may be a skills gap, a knowledge gap, or a network gap. Your value proposition is to build them a bridge, or jump across it yourself so that they don't have to.

People sometimes talk about being a "market disruptor" or even a "market destabilizer." But you don't need to do anything quite so dramatic. You just need to lead your clients from A to B. In my company, the gap I bridge for my clients is the chasm between corporate people and finance people.

The corporate people don't know what's going on in the economy at large. At McKinsey, I remember when a very senior partner thought the price of oil was $30 higher than it was. He hadn't been keeping track of the price. But I had. So now I sell that kind of information to the people who don't have it. The finance people also don't know what's going on in the corporate world. I tell them. I bridge that gap on both sides. I'm able to do that because I'm one of the rare few who understand both business and finance.

What two worlds do *you* straddle? That's your value proposition. Narrowing down your value proposition is all about finding your *unique* skillset.

There's an important distinction between *blue oceans* and *red oceans*. A blue ocean is a business niche with few competitors. A red ocean is a business niche with many competitors; they're at each other's necks and it's getting bloody. A red ocean is a tough place to succeed if you're just starting out. You want to be in a blue ocean, the place no one's been before. The way to find that blue ocean is to figure out what you provide that no one else does.

This concept is put forward in the book *Blue Ocean Strategy*.

Dip your toes before jumping in.

Of course, you might have a unique skillset that no one wants. You're the only person in the world who is an expert on both Egyptian hieroglyphics and supply chain management, but who cares? No one needs a *preneur* to take them entre those two things. How can you tell if your value proposition is one that people will actually pay for?

The best way is to just try it, but at a low level of commitment so that if it doesn't work out, the repo man isn't going to tow your car away. This can be easily done if your business is low-capital. A *low-capital* business is one that has low startup costs, one that you can get off the ground without spending much money. These tend to be service-based or advisory businesses, ones that you can run from home or online. For instance, a one-person copyediting business is a very low-capital business. It's literally just you on a laptop in your spare bedroom.

In contrast, a *high-capital* business has high startup costs. For instance, a restaurant is a high-capital business, because you have to rent some real estate, furnish and decorate the place, and buy high-quality kitchen equipment before you sell even a single meal. A cell phone network is an *extremely* high-capital business, because you have to build lots of cell towers before anyone would possibly pay for your service. The less money you can spend to start, the better. If your startup costs are very low, you can try several different businesses before finding the one that works for you, without burning through all your savings.

The only sensible way to build a high-capital business is to go very slowly, with low-capital beginnings. You might want to be the next Steve Jobs, but even he started in his garage with a couple of screwdrivers. Shark Tank judge Mark Cuban has gone on record saying that he started out selling garbage bags door to door.

Telecommuting from home is a great option. Instead of *spending* money on overhead for your out-of-home office, you're *saving* money on a tax write-off for your home office. Just because your business is based out of your house doesn't mean it's not a major player in your industry. When I started Prestige Economics, my office was a granite countertop in my kitchen, in an $800/month apartment. You can see my office just to the right of my cooktop.

That's about as low-capital as it gets, and you know what? I was ranked better than Goldman. I was #1 in the world at a number of different forecasts, beating out big financial firms, all from a kitchen counter.

Keep an eye on your benchmarks.

Let's say you've decided on your business idea. Great, but before you launch it, you need to ask yourself five questions about getting this business off the ground. They are all about what I call your "runway" — the amount of money and time you need for your business to take off.

QUESTION 1: RUNWAY. HOW MUCH MONEY AND TIME DO YOU NEED TO GET YOUR BUSINESS OFF THE GROUND?

If a plane doesn't have a long enough runway, it won't build up enough speed to take flight. The same is true of your business. Your runway is the amount of time you need to start turning a profit, to start making a living off of your business.

To give you a rough sense of how long your runway needs to be, think about this: the IRS is not known as a generous or forgiving organization, but even they give people three whole years of being self-employed before they ask for proof that they are turning a profit. That's right: you can claim self-employment write-offs left and right on your taxes for three years without actually having a profitable business. That's because it often takes new business owners that many years to actually start making money.

The IRS *expects* you to be bleeding from your eyes for three years.

If you turn a profit in less than that, you're doing really well.

Your runway is the most critical number you must calculate before starting a business, and it consists of two parts: investment capital and living capital. So, in order to understand your runway, you need to be able to answer two other questions.

QUESTION 2: INVESTMENT CAPITAL. HOW MUCH DO YOU NEED TO INVEST?

This is a critical part of your runway. It includes all of your business startup costs — ranging from nothing for a virtual business that you run out of your home, to tens of thousands of dollars for a restaurant or the like. Your expenses might include travel, attending conferences, software, hardware, staffing, and office equipment.

You need to have this money in the bank, because no one is going to loan it to you before you can turn a profit.

QUESTION 3: LIVING CAPITAL. HOW MUCH DO YOU NEED TO SURVIVE PERSONALLY?

Don't forget that while you're building your company, you also need to be living. Calculate how much you need in order to simply survive during the time you are starting your company and haven't made any money on it.

Once you have a rough idea of the breakdown of the costs associated with your runway, ask yourself two more questions:

QUESTION 4: CAN YOU LENGTHEN YOUR RUNWAY BY CUTTING COSTS OR INCREASING CASH FLOW?

The longer the runway, the greater the chance of success. Starting a business may not be the time to buy a house — that down payment will cut a huge chunk out of your runway money.

Lowering your expenses will lengthen your runway. Also, don't be afraid to liquidate your IRA if you believe in the business and have proof of concept. After all, this may be the lowest tax rate you'll ever pay on that money, because right now it's the only money you're making.

QUESTION 5: WHAT ARE YOUR BREAKING POINTS?

The final question you need to answer before starting a business is at what point you'll cut your losses and close up shop. Stock traders always say that you should never get into a trade until you know the point at which you'll get out. The same is true of starting a business. Economists talk about the fallacy of sunk costs. It's the mistaken idea that if you've invested a ton of money, time, and emotional energy into something, you need to keep investing in it until it pays off, so that you haven't wasted everything you already put in.

It's a very dangerous idea, because it makes people sink more and more of their resources into a bad idea.

I've seen plenty of people who get emotionally attached to their businesses and keep them going longer than they should. Don't be one of those people. If your business isn't working out, there's no shame in closing up.

Once you've answered these five questions, you can calculate if you have enough time and money to make your business successful.

When I started my business, I had $125,000 in the bank. I estimated that over a three-year period, I would need to put $60,000 into startup costs, plus $60,000 per year in living expenses if I cut my costs by moving to Austin. This gave me three years as a runway, but just barely. That is not a ton of time, but it's enough to have a reasonable chance of success.

Fortunately, it paid off.

If you don't have enough time and money to make it work, you might want to start your business in a smaller, lower-capital form. You can just dip your toes in, in a way that is so small that you can keep your current job until your business takes off, and have an essentially infinite runway.

If you start out with a few "anchor clients" — clients that consistently give you contracts — you can break even and stay afloat for many years, and that gives you a very long runway for making your business truly thrive. I did not have any anchor clients when I started my business, and I still managed to make it work. But it would have been a lot easier with anchor clients.

Buckle up.

If you like risk, volatility, and Vegas casino gambling, then you probably have what it takes to be an entrepreneur! Starting a business is like putting your life savings on red and hoping the wheel spins the right way. Some days you think you're going to be a millionaire and other days you think about which relatives you can move in with.

It's a scary, stressful process, which is why this isn't the only strategy I'm talking about in this book. It's not for everyone.

But with high risk comes high rewards. When people ask me if I have children, I say, "No, but I have a company." Your company is your baby. It might be an ugly baby. It might ruin your sleep. It might need to be fed at 4:00 a.m. It'll probably stress you out. But it's yours and you have to love it.

You need an iron stomach.

For months or years, you'll watch your bank account inch slowly down. It's free fall with no parachute.

Remember that $125,000 runway I mentioned before?

I ran it down to just $4,000 before I started making serious money. If your clients are corporations, it might take 60 to 90 days for you to get paid, and that feels like an awfully long time when you're just a couple of months from the end of your runway.

You must be adaptive.

A business is alive, and it must change and develop and grow in order to survive. And it may change so much that it becomes unrecognizable by the time it is successful. You might have a perfect vision of a certain product or service, but if that's not what people are buying, you need to move on and follow the money.

When I started my business, I gave out my market research for free. I did this because I thought of it as just a way of building my brand. I didn't realize that this was my core product. Now I sell some of those market reports for tens of thousands of dollars each. Furthermore, not only do I not give away my research for free any more, but I find it insulting when people who have no intention of buying anything try to pump me for free information.

It took me a while to learn the difference between a real business lead and someone looking for free stuff. But my big takeaway is the same: Give away a little to actual potential clients. But don't give anything to people who are wasting your time.

Be hungry. But be patient.

If you're not hungry, you will not eat. And while being both hungry and patient seems contradictory — and really tough to master — it's necessary. I scared off potential clients early on because I was too aggressive. I showed too clearly how much I needed their business. And I did *need* their business — but if they know that, sometimes they won't give it to you.

> **CHECKLIST OF CONSIDERATIONS IF YOU ARE GOING TO START A BUSINESS**
>
> - Am I starting this business while the opportunity cost is low?
> - Do I have a unique value proposition?
> - Do I have potential clients, especially anchor clients?
> - Have I proved my concept at a low level of commitment?
> - How long a runway do I need?
> - How long a runway can I afford?
> - What can I do to lengthen my runway?
> - At what point will I cut and run?
> - Can I handle the stress?
> - What are my goals for year one, two, and three?
> - What is my backup plan if it doesn't work out?

Ask for money, and ask for the right amount.

If you start a business, you are now a salesperson. Whatever it is you're actually *doing* — building furniture, making artisanal soap, providing tax advice — you are first and foremost a salesperson.

If your background isn't in sales, this can be hard to get used to.

It's a very strange thing: you're not the guy on the side of the road saying "Give me some cash," but you're totally the guy on the side of the road saying, "Give me some cash."

When I started my company, my background was in analysis, not sales. I had to sign up for a Master's degree in Negotiation in order to learn how to do that side of my job.

So embrace it.

Do as the salespeople do.

Salespeople are always closing. Salespeople steer clear of underpricing. If you undersell yourself, if you accept less than you're worth just to get a contract, you could be stuck with that low rate for a long time.

Your client knows you're willing to work for X, so they're not going to want to pay you X + 1. When you do try to raise your rates, you're likely to lose that customer.

So you need to make sure you don't underprice yourself at the start. I began by handing out my company's market research reports for free, and when I went from free to charging for it, I lost 95 percent of my clients right away.

Then again, I also went from making no money, to making some money.

Set measurable and reasonable goals.

You need to know how well your business is doing. The obvious way is to look at your bottom line: your profits and losses. Your company is not going to be one of the Big Three any time soon, you're not going to start Facebook or Uber overnight, but if you can increase your gross income by 50 percent over the previous year, that's real progress.

This kind of realistic goal keeps you motivated without putting your head in the clouds. When your business is still a baby, profit and loss are not enough to measure your success. The fact that you're losing money at the beginning doesn't mean things are going poorly.

After all, you're still on your runway.

You need non-financial ways of measuring how well you're doing. Corporations like to call these KPIs: Key Performance Indicators.

In the early days of my company, my KPI was days on the road. If I was traveling a lot to meet with clients, I was doing well. In 2012, when Prestige was three years old, I was on the road over 240 days that year. That's crazy, but it told me that I was hustling and building.

Drop the bad apples.

Look at the chart in Figure 8-2. It shows you which clients are worth it, and which aren't.

Figure 8-2: Prioritizing Clients[2]

Client Matrix	High-effort client	Low-effort client
High-paying client	These are good clients. Keep them. Try to move them into the high-pay/low-effort bucket.	These are the best clients. Keep them happy!
Low-paying client	Drop these clients. They are not worth the effort.	These are good clients. Keep them. Try to move them into the high-pay/low-effort bucket.

This may seem obvious, but you'd be surprised how often people ignore this.

If you're starting a business, you probably have some low-paying, high-effort clients. These are people who value you but don't pay you much.

Trust me, they're not worth it.

You'll never get ahead with this kind of poor ROI. One of the advantages of owning your own company is that you can fire a bad client, so do it.

Bad employees and business partners are as toxic as bad clients. If you run a successful business, there are going to be a lot of people who want some of your secret sauce.

Some of those are good and trustworthy people, and some of them are not. Your business is your baby, and you don't want somebody that's going to play football with your baby. So be careful about who you work with.

The deal that ruins you isn't the deal you missed — it's the deal you shouldn't have done. The deal you shouldn't have done is the deal with bad people. Whether they're clients, partners, or staff, drop them now.

Have a backup plan (or three).

Your business might fail. That's just the reality of entrepreneurship. Eight in 10 businesses fail in the first 18 months. If you think you're somehow exempt from that — if you don't have a solid plan for what to do if it happens — then you shouldn't start a business. Backup plans come in many shapes and sizes.

Backup plan #1 is that list of five to 10 people you can call today to get a job tomorrow. In the early years of Prestige, I had that list posted next to my desk in case it all went sideways.

Backup plan #2 is to liquidate your assets. You should write down everything you own that you could sell without ruining your life and the lives of your spouse and children.

When I had burned down my savings from $125,000 to just $4,000, you better believe I was thinking about that list really hard.

Some of things on my list were: my car; my cufflinks collection; an ivory chess set I was given by my uncle as a college graduation gift. I would have hated to part with an item of personal significance like that, but it wouldn't have ruined my life. For other people, your list might include real estate or your IRA. (My IRA wasn't on my liquidation list only because I'd already cashed it in to get that $125,000 runway fund.)

Backup plan #3 might be: your spouse rejoins the workforce; you move back in with your parents; you move back in with your grown children. These might be unthinkable options. But even the unthinkable is worth thinking about.

Be kind to yourself.

Finally, be kind to yourself. Starting a business is hard. It's stressful. It's scary. It might not work out. Give it a go, in a smart way, but if doesn't work out — if you're not making money or if you just don't like the stress of going it alone — there's no shame in quitting.

It's important to know when to fish and when to cut bait.

After all, you don't want to get pulled overboard!

CHAPTER SUMMARY

- You can build your skills or you can build a business.

- Get your employer to pay for new skills.

- Find cheap or free learning opportunities.

- Recessions are a great time to start a business.

- Look for low-capital opportunities.

- Find your unique value proposition.

- Know your runway, your breaking point, and your exit plan.

CHAPTER 9

INVEST

MAKE YOUR MONEY MAKE MONEY

If you're going into a recession with some cash in hand, you're lucky. But don't get lazy. You need to know where to put that money so that your money can work for you. Invest in a business you've already started. Invest in your kids' education — there's a surprising twist here about why. If you know what you're doing, invest in the stock market. But before you do, keep a few very basic principles in mind.

Don't invest money you can't afford to lose.

My uncle was a Wall Street stockbroker for Charles Schwab in the 1980s. These were heady times. The economy was picking up after the early '80s. Then came Black Monday in 1987. Markets around the world crashed. It was a computer glitch. Traders essentially just walked away from their computers, unable to transact.

My uncle was working that day, and from that day forward, he always told me, "Don't invest money that you're afraid to lose."

That's true whether you're investing in the stock market or in your own business. Don't liquidate your children's college fund. Don't take out a second mortgage to buy leveraged calls. Don't bet the house.

Invest only in things you understand.

If you watch house-themed reality shows, it's easy to start thinking that anyone can make a cool $50,000 just by buying a house, doing a few renovations, and selling it again at a profit a few months later ("flipping" it).

Some shows will even make it seem like you don't need to add any value to the house to make a profit. Buy a house, wait six months for the price to increase, then flip it.

The truth is, these are also great ways to *lose* money. There is no shortage of house flippers who really got burned when the real-estate bubble burst in 2008. Remember that whatever you are investing in, you are competing with folks who do nothing all day but study all the ins and outs of that market. So only invest in things that you understand.

Don't be a house flipper unless you learn the real estate game well, and make a business of it. It's not something you can enter casually.

Of course, buying a house *is* a great idea, not because you can flip it two weeks later, but because you can live in it! When I lived in Charlotte, I bought a condo when the housing market was really hot. A woman asked me how much my condo was worth. I said, "I have no idea." She was surprised and almost indignant. She said,

"How could you not know how much your condo is worth?" I told her, "I don't know because I *live* here. I didn't buy it in order to sell it. I bought it to live in it. The mortgage is okay and the condo is nice, so I'm happy to live here."

Unless you really know what you're doing, that's how you should think about your house. The same goes for anything else you buy.

Invest in many different things.

People like to say that the three most important factors for a successful restaurant are location, location, and location. In the same way, the three most important factors for successful investment are diversification, diversification, diversification.

That's Investing 101.

If you invest in just one thing, you'd make a ton of money if that thing does well, but you'd also lose everything if it does poorly. Plus, losing everything feels infinitely worse than it would feel merely to have missed the chance to make a lot of money. The wider the variety of things you invest in, the safer you are.

INVEST IN YOUR BUSINESS

You probably don't have a million dollars to become an "angel" investor in some biotech startup. But maybe you have $20,000 to sink into your own small business. Redecorate your restaurant. Fly to Europe to visit some potential clients. Buy some more Facebook or Google ads. Pay a professional to spruce up that website of yours that just screams 1999. Whatever it is, a relatively small investment in your existing business can have a high ROI and pay back many times over.

What does the smart money do?

Rather than sinking a dollar in the stock market, the smart money sinks it into private companies. This is what the smart money does, and it's what you should do too, if you can. You should invest money in your own company. You can't control what IBM does, but you can control what your own company does. This goes under the heading of investing in things you understand. There's nothing you understand better than your own business.

Trust me on this one. I'm a Certified Valuation Analyst®, which means that I have professional training in deciding just how many dollars a company is worth. So I can tell you a few things about the value of investing in your own company, rather than the stock market.

A big, publicly traded company has a very volatile price. Since anyone can buy a share in the company, the share price is going to be vulnerable to people (and computers) buying and selling shares for all kinds of reasons.

The company could be doing well and turning a profit quarter after quarter, but the stock price might still crash just because a bunch of computers trading with each other based on algorithms get into a sell-off frenzy.

Suddenly, overnight, the company might be "worth" nothing, even though it has been selling lots of products and making lots of money.

This is especially likely to happen during a recession In contrast, a small, privately owned company — like your business — isn't exposed to such crazy volatility. Its value isn't determined by what a bunch of day traders and computer algorithms are buying and selling it for at any particular millisecond.

The company's value is determined entirely by how well it's actually doing — how much profit it's making. In fancy language: its valuation is stable. When a recession rolls around, you might lose some customers, but the value of your company isn't going to tank like it would in the world of publicly traded companies.

The upshot: when you invest in a big public corporation, you can go broke even if the company is making lots of money.

But when you invest in your own small business, you'll never go broke by making a profit. Investing in your own business is therefore a great way to recession-proof your life.

That's the magic of investing in your own business. There's another bit of magic, too. If you invest in your business and then sell it, you won't just be paid for the money your business is bringing in this year, you'll be paid for all the money it is *expected* to make in the future.

Let's say that you're bringing in $50,000 a year at your business. If you're likely to continue making that $50,000 a year for the next 20 years, your business isn't worth just $50,000, it's worth $50,000 multiplied by 20 — a million dollars.

Of course, the buyer isn't going to pay that entire million dollar figure, because he wants to make a profit, and money made in the future is never an entirely sure thing. Even so, you'll get paid much more than $50,000 for your $50,000-per-year business.

Depending on the industry, you might be paid three times your yearly earnings, or five times, or eight times, or even 10 or 12 times. You're getting paid for money you haven't earned yet.

Fantastic.

The multiple that you're paid is higher if your business is clearly a "going concern" — a moneymaker that will continue to generate revenue in the future. A great way to prove to potential buyers that your business is a going concern is to land some multi-year contracts.

Plus, if you can increase your company's profits, you increase the value of your company — and its future selling price.

There are smart phone apps that have sold for billions of dollars before earning a single penny.

How is that possible? It's possible because the buyers expect the app to have a certain number of users and expect each user to pay a certain amount of money.

The buyer is paying for what *might* happen. I've gotten offers for my company. I've never taken one, but it's a good feeling to know that, someday, if I want to, I could cash in overnight on all the money my company is *going* to make.

That's the beauty of investing in your own business.

DRILL #16: CAN I AFFORD TO START A BUSINESS?

Answer these two questions:

1. How much money do you currently have in different investment accounts?

_____

2. How much of that money can you afford to lose?

_____

If the answer to question one is more than the answer to question two, then you need to stop. Simply put: *You should never invest money that you cannot afford to lose.*

INVEST IN YOUR CHILDREN'S EDUCATION

If you have kids, you love them more than anything in the world. You invest in their education so that they will be healthy, happy, and prosperous in life. You do it for *them*, not for yourself. You do it without expecting anything back. You do it without even thinking about making a profit. Right?

Not quite! Of course you should help your kids out in life because you love them. But there are also some very good selfish reasons to invest in your kids' success, and it's important to think about what they are. To understand why investing in your kids' education is such a good investment for *yourself*, we need to talk about retirement.

A lot of people are still in denial about this.

In 2015, 62 percent of Social Security recipients received at least half of their income from Social Security.[1] And many Americans are still banking on the idea that they will be able to live off of Social Security in their retirements way into the future. That's a horrible fallacy, and the people who fall prey to it are going to get wise the hard way.

Plus, that's just Social Security. Medicare is in even worse shape.

When entitlements dry up, how will old people survive?

The way they did for thousands of years before the welfare state — by relying on their families.

When it comes to retirement, the past is the future. We're going to become more family-oriented out of necessity. We're going to rely less on the government and more on our children, like we did for most of our history as a species. When I lived in Germany in the late 1990s, I had a roommate from Eritrea. He was one of 21 children. His parents had 21 kids in the hopes that at least *one* of them wouldn't turn out to be a total jerk, and would take care of them in their old age.

This is why you should invest in your children's education. This is why investing in your children's education — their professional success in life — is the very best investment you could ever make, the investment with the highest ROI. That's because when you're old, it's your children who will take care of you. There's an old joke which isn't a joke at all: "Pick a nice college for your kids, because they're going to pick your retirement home."

While you're at it, make sure your kids know you love them.

DON'T INVEST IN THE STOCK MARKET (UNLESS...)
Investing in your business means investing in something you control and you understand. Investing in your children's education means investing in their future — and yours. Investing in the stock market, on the other hand, is like gambling in Vegas.

It's like playing craps, roulette, or poker. Your biggest return on investment is the stress of watching your stock prices go up and down all day. So the first thing I'll say about actively investing in the stock market is: be very, very careful.

A little knowledge is a dangerous thing.

To understand why investing in the stock market can be such a bad idea, you need to understand something called the monkey line.

There's something called the infinite monkey theorem, which says that if you put a hundred monkeys in a room with a hundred typewriters, and if you wait long enough, they will type *Hamlet*. Now, the statistics around this are infinitely unlikely, but if you put those monkeys in a room with two big Jim Cramer buttons, one that says "BUY" and one that says "SELL," they could trade in financial markets — and they would likely perform better than the average person.

Let's imagine that you've hired a monkey to make all your investment decisions. The monkey has no idea what he's doing. He doesn't even know what the stock market is. He's just hitting buttons randomly, and when he hits the button that says "BUY," you buy a share, and when he hits the button that says "SELL," you sell a share.

Sometimes the monkey gets lucky and hits "BUY" or "SELL" at just the right time, and you make a bunch of money. Sometimes the monkey gets unlucky and hits "BUY" or "SELL" at the worst possible time, and you lose a bunch of money. It's random. So overall, with a monkey as your investment consultant, you break even. Win some, lose some, and it'll average out to whatever the stock market is doing overall.

In other words, you can expect the monkey to be right 50 percent of the time. And that's the monkey line: the amount of money you'd make from the stock market if you make decisions completely at random. Naturally, an investor wants to be above the monkey line, and wants to avoid being below the monkey line.

In Figure 9-1, the x-axis is *information* — the farther to the right you get, the more information you have. And the y-axis is, where 50% represents the average returns a monkey would get with no information. That's why the monkey line is that horizontal line in the middle, at the 50/50 break-even point.

Figure 9-1: The Monkey Line

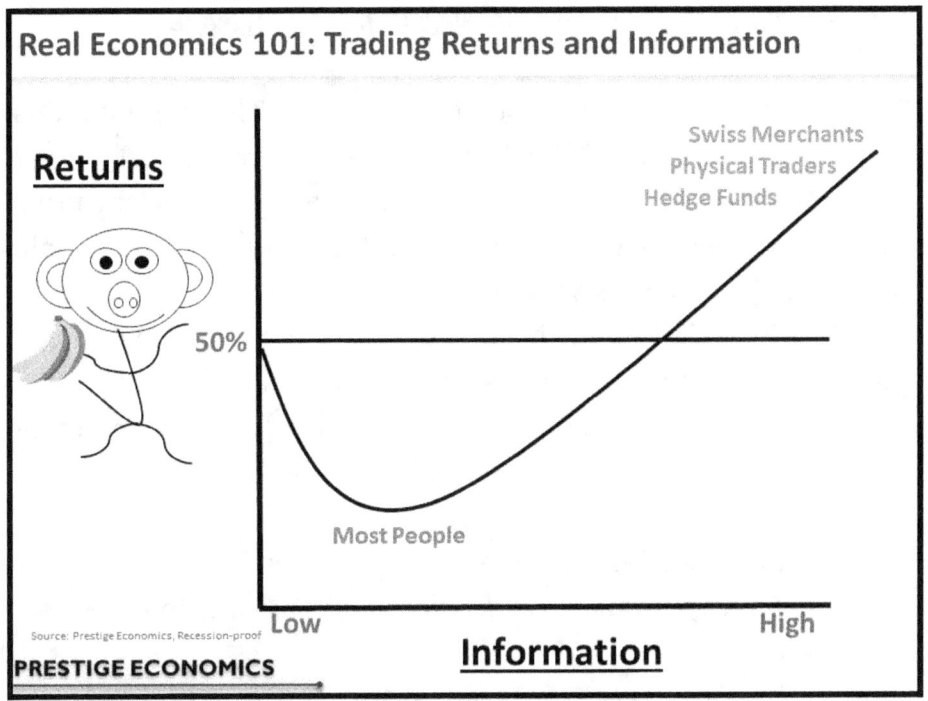

The graph shows that if you know nothing about playing the stock market — i.e. if you make decisions like a monkey — then you'll be right at the monkey line (50 percent). That makes sense.

The graph also shows that if you're a really savvy investor with a lot of experience and knowledge, you'll be able to play the stock market and come out well *above* the monkey line. That also makes sense.

The funny, surprising part of the graph, however, is this: if you know *a little bit* about the stock market, if you have *a little bit* of skill and knowledge, guess where you'll end up? You'll end up *below* the monkey line! That's right: you'll be worse off than if you just hired the monkey. As the saying goes: a little knowledge is a dangerous thing. I call it *dangerous half-knowledge.*

The reason for this requires some explanation. Think about it this way: all you've got is *TIME Magazine* and *The Wall Street Journal* and something you read on some guy's blog about gold price fluctuations. Meanwhile the big investment firms have people like me on retainer, as well as scores and scores of really smart people with PhDs. All of those people are doing nothing all day but using the most sophisticated equipment and techniques to predict where the market will go. That's who you're competing against.

By the time a small-fry investor has read the financial news in *The Wall Street Journal* or *The Economist*, it's already too late.

After all, *The Economist* comes out once a week.

Whatever they are reporting happened at least a couple days ago. The big dogs got the news within seconds, and within minutes they were doing all the right trades to make a ton of money on that news. By the time you hear about it, on your way home from work or on the nightly news, the party is over.

If General Motors took a hit because of an unexpected auto recall, you're now selling off your stock in that company when it might already be at its lowest point. If Apple's stock soared because of stronger-than-expected third quarter earnings, you're probably buying that stock when it's already at its highest point. Either way, you've lost money, because you knew a little bit.

These days, breaking financial news causes exaggerated stock price changes. It's not just a handful of hedge funds or investors who watch these market shifts — it's individuals, central banks, everyone. Once a stock price starts to drop, it picks up its own momentum. An object in motion stays in motion. By the time you've heard about it on CNBC, the stock has already dived made the worst possible trade. The market moves so quickly that if you're getting the news just a little bit later than the big players, you're already too late. As a small player, the only time you'll know more about the market than the big players is if you work at a company and have insider knowledge. You might know that the company is about to announce some exciting new product. But if you trade on that knowledge, you could very well experience what people in finance and trading refer to as a *liberty-reducing event*. The FBI will come by with some special jewelry. Congratulations: before you knew too little, but now you know too much.

Three rules to get above the monkey line.

Now that I've scared you about the stock market, I'll soften my message a bit. You can invest in the stock market, as long as you do it very carefully, very conservatively, by taking advantage of the expertise that others have, and following certain rules. Plus, knowing what the big guys are watching can put you in a much better position.

The First Rule: *Buy bundles of stocks, not individual stocks.*

Bundles of stocks go by names like mutual funds and ETFs (exchange-traded funds, a mutual fund that trades more like a stock). They include shares in many different companies so that if a few companies do poorly, you'll hardly notice the difference.

These bundles are products that professional investors — the kind of people who know how to trade way above the monkey line — put together and sell to people like you, so that you don't need to work out the details for yourself.

Most people wouldn't try to fix their own furnace, because if you do it wrong, it might explode in your face. In the same way, you probably shouldn't choose your own portfolio of stocks.

You're better off seeking the professional services of someone who really knows how to do that. Buying a bundle of stocks, like a mutual fund, is how you do that. It's the financial equivalent of hiring a plumber rather than messing with the pipes yourself and flooding the house.

If you want *some* involvement in your investment decisions, consider buying ETFs in particular industries. Let's say that you have a good feeling about the auto industry. It would be foolish to buy stock in just one auto company.

You might get a recall on a part. There might be an internal scandal or lawsuit, and suddenly the stock price plunges. All kinds of weird things can happen.

So if you feel strongly about autos, invest in an ETF in the auto industry as a whole. It may not be as diversified as a mutual fund, which could include stocks from all kinds of industries, but it's much more diversified than investing in just one single company.

The Second Rule: *Buy in bust times, not boom times.*

It's a bit counterintuitive, but it makes sense once you think about it. The boom times are actually the scariest times to invest. If everything's looking rosy, that's when you should get nervous. The bubble might burst at any moment, and you'll lose your money. If, on the other hand, you buy into the stock market during a recession, the only way forward is up.

There's an old saying, misattributed to lots of people: "The time to buy is when there's blood in the street."

Look at the graph below. The Dow Jones Industrial Average is an index of 30 stocks. It's used as an indicator of how well the U.S. stock market is doing as a whole. In October 2007, it was at 14,165. By March 2009, it had gone all the way down to 6,549. Ask yourself, would you rather have bought when the Dow was at 14,165, or when it was at 6,549?

The answer should be obvious: buy low.

Shares are cheap during a recession, so this is the time when you can afford to take on riskier trading. This is when you might consider doing what is called "active trading" — buying and selling individual stocks.

Figure 9-2: The Dow[2]

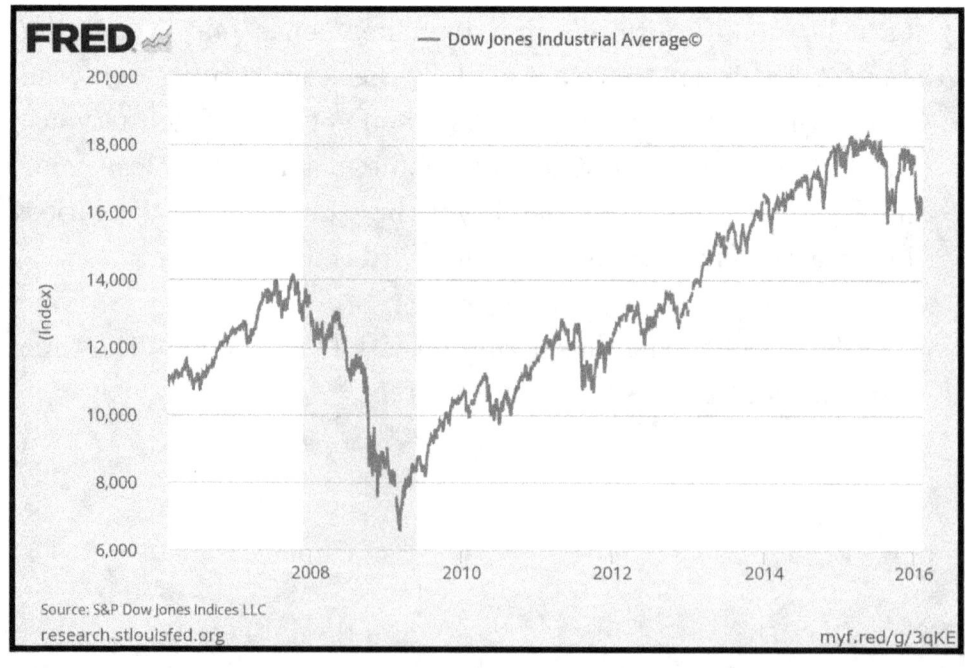

For a nonprofessional, a recession is the only time you should consider doing this. Remember recession-proof (acyclical) vs. recession-prone (procyclical) industries, from Chapter 2?

Think about that when you're choosing your investments.

After the worst of a recession, when recovery seems to be around the corner, it may be a good time to buy stock in a procyclical industry. After all, it will likely recover when the economy improves. This is usually true of industrials, for example. Then, after the economy is doing its best, you may want to sell that investment and diversify into some recession-proof investments.

After all, with markets — and GDP — what goes up, comes down.

In a recession, you might not want to buy stock in a recession-proof industry. After all, it probably saw its biggest gains when the recession hit, and it might have much less upside in a recovery.

To take full advantage of the business cycle, you'll want to work with a Certified Financial Planner® (CFP®) to readjust your investments in line with the booms and busts.

In up years, you may wish to rotate some of your money into blue chip bonds, cash, or money market accounts. But in down years, you might benefit from moving some of that money into the stock market.

The Third Rule: *Retire at the right time.*

That means retiring during a boom year, when the stock markets are rocking. That way, you're converting your shares into the highest possible fixed income, which could keep you financially supported for the rest of your life, no matter what the stock market does.

Of course, retiring at the right time is easy if you were born in the right year. Be born in the right year, graduate in the right year, retire in the right year, and you'll have it made in the shade. "I'd rather be lucky than good" is the motto here. Unfortunately, no one decides when they were born.

If you weren't lucky enough to be born exactly 67 years before a great retirement year, you still have some wiggle room.

You can retire at 62, 67, 70, or any time in between, and that window will give you a full set of options for which part of the business cycle you'll retire into. If you're 63 and the economy is hot, you might to think about retiring early.

After the Great Recession, people postponed their retirements in the United States. Now, after the onset of the COVID-19 pandemic, it may also be the case that the 50 and up crowd could stay even longer in the labor force — and at a greater percentage than ever before — in order to make up for financial losses and avoid retiring into a tough economy, when investments may have lost value or are at risk of remaining weak.

CHAPTER SUMMARY

- When it comes to retirement, the past is the future. We're going to become more family-oriented out of necessity.

- Invest in the business you know best: your own.

- Invest in your kids, because you'll depend on them when you're old.

- Invest in the stock market with caution; a little knowledge is a dangerous thing.

- You should never invest money that you cannot afford to lose.

CHAPTER 10

NOW WHAT?

REASSESS YOUR OPTIONS

I've told you how to prepare, how to dig in, how to hide, how to run, how to build, and how to invest — six strategies for recession-proofing your life.

Now what? Which of those strategies is right for you?

The first thing you need to do is to revisit that SWOT (Strengths, Weaknesses, Opportunities, Threats) analysis I told you about in Chapter 3. Redo your SWOT analysis based on everything you've learned in this book. By now you should be able to see some strengths and opportunities that you didn't appreciate before. You should also be able to see some weaknesses and threats that might once have caught you off-guard.

Your SWOT analysis will change as you do. It will change as your knowledge of all the good and bad in yourself and your environment increases.

RECESSION-PROOF YOUR LIFE (REPRISE)

Let's review the six strategies you've learned about in this book. You may find that, now that you've redone your SWOT analysis, a strategy which seemed impossible before now seems possible, and even desirable!

Strategy 1: Prepare

What does it mean? It means get your head in the game, get hungry, anticipate the next recession, build your resume, and ask yourself what you're willing to do when the chips are down, and what you're not. You're reading this book, so you've already taken a great first step toward preparing.

Who should do it? Everyone! This is the foundational step, and no matter your particular situation, you've got to do it.

Strategy 2: Dig In

What does it mean? This means doing everything possible to stay in your current job, company, or industry. It means clinging on like a barnacle. It means becoming that indispensable employee who keeps his or her job even when other people in the same situation are losing theirs.

Who should do it? This strategy is best for individuals who aren't able to change their life situations easily. If you're the sole breadwinner for your family, if you have an elderly parent to take care of, if it's extremely important to you to stay in the town where you grew up and where all your friends and family live, then this is the option for you.

Strategy 3: Hide

What does it mean? This means taking refuge from the recession, either by staying in school (or going back to school) until the economy is looking up, or by finding a safe-haven job in a recession-proof industry.

Who should do it? It's easiest to go back to school if you're young, but, really, anyone can do it. As for finding a job in a recession-proof industry, that will depend on whether you have those skills. If you have chops in education, healthcare, and government, hunkering down in those stable sectors is a good option.

Strategy 4: Run

What does it mean? It means physically relocating to a geographical location where prospects are better. It can also mean pivoting out of an industry or a company that is going down the tubes. It's about focusing on what you're running toward, not what you're running away from.

Who should do it? Moving physically is easiest if you are unencumbered. That often means that you're young and don't have a spouse or kids, but it might also mean that you and your spouse are empty-nesters looking for a new adventure.

Strategy 5: Build

What does it mean? It means two things: build your skills, or build your own business. Both of them are investments in You, Inc.

Who should do it? Everyone can build their skills. As for building a business, it's generally best for someone with a long runway — the amount of time you can afford to spend building your business before it turns a profit. People with long runways tend to be people who either have a spouse who makes a steady income, people who have a chunk of money in the bank that they can afford to lose, or people who have various assets they can sell off to finance their entrepreneurial adventure.

Strategy 6: Invest
What does it mean? It means putting money into an existing business to grow it, helping pay for your kids' education, or investing very, very carefully in the stock market. It doesn't mean buying and selling individual stocks — unless you really know what you're doing.

Who should do it? Anyone with kids should absolutely be investing in their education, not just for their sake but for your sake! You'll depend on them when you're older. Anyone with some money in the bank should put it into a safe mutual fund. Only the brave, the savvy, or the foolish will engage in active trading.

EVERYONE CAN DO SOMETHING
Be as proactive as you can be. "Proactive" has become overused and has lost a lot of its meaning. What it really means is acting before something happens, in anticipation of it. "Reactive," on the other hand, means acting after something happens, as a reaction to it. You want to be proactive in the face of a coming recession, in every possible way.

Proactive strategies might be: Hiding in school by signing up for a graduate program in anticipation of a coming economic downturn; or Investing in your children's education with the expectation that you'll rely on them in your retirement. These are all things you do before the recession hits, and because you have that leg up on the economic downturn, you're in a good position to weather it well.

But really, any of the six strategies can be proactive, if you're doing them right. Running can be a proactive strategy, if you're bailing early from a doomed company, industry, or region. Even Digging In can be a proactive strategy, if you're building your skills in the up years so that you'll be unfireable in the down years.

I wrote this book to help you be as proactive as possible. I wrote it so that you'll have that Plan B, Plan C, and Plan D in the hopper, all ready to go, before everything goes south.

You need to have that conversation with your family now — the conversation about what you'll do in a recession. It might freak them out to hear that tough times are coming.

But trust me, it'll freak them out even more if you put it off and then say, "Tough times are here!"

It'll reassure them to know that you've got a plan. It'll reassure you, too. One of the worst impacts of a recession is the stress and anxiety it can inflict on people. Having a plan calms that anxiety.

Every situation is different. Not everything is possible for everyone.

But no matter who you are and what your life is like, you have options as you face down this charging bull. No one can do everything, but everyone can do *something*.

CONCLUSION

YOU'RE IN CONTROL

A recession is here. Some will give up. Some will sink into depression. Some will end up on the street. These will be casualties, and they will number in the millions. They will understand in a real and terrible way why economics is called *the dismal science*.

You don't have to be one of these people. You have foreknowledge. You have self-knowledge. You have a strategy, a game plan. You know your options.

You're jumping at opportunities, leveraging strengths, heading off threats, and patching up weaknesses. You're making the bold choices — leaping to a brand-new industry, packing up to a new city, starting a business that is uniquely *you* — that others would never dare. You're going to survive and thrive in the next downturn. You're going to run with the bull markets. You're going to get some dirt-encrusted drool on your leg, but you're going to get through it — and when the boom comes back, you'll be in a great position to take full advantage of it. That's the best part of grabbing the bull by the horns!

ENDNOTES

Chapter 1

1. Data for U.S. ISM Manufacturing, Chinese Caixin Manufacturing PMI, and Eurozone Manufacturing PMI retrieved on 1 July 2020 from www.tradingeconomics.com.
2. World Economic Outlook. (24 June 2020). IMF. Retrieved on 1 July 2020 from https://www.imf.org/en/Publications/WEO/Issues/2020/06/24/WEOUpdateJune2020.
3. World Economic Outlook. (14 April 2020). IMF. Retrieved on 1 July 2020 from https://www.imf.org/en/Publications/WEO/Issues/2020/04/14/weo-april-2020
4. World Economic Outlook. (24 June 2020). IMF. Retrieved on 1 July 2020 from https://www.imf.org/en/Publications/WEO/Issues/2020/06/24/WEOUpdateJune2020.
5. Unemployment Insurance Weekly Claims. (25 June 2020). Department of Labor. Retrieved on 1 July 2020 from https://www.dol.gov/ui/data.pdf.

Chapter 2

1. Regional unemployment statistics sourced from ww.bls.gov.
2. Data for U.S. ISM Manufacturing sourced from www.tradingeconomics.com.
3. Stanford University. Retrieved on 15 February 2016 from WEB.STANFORD.EDU/~CY10/PUBLIC/LOSING_A_JOB.PDF
4. IMF. Retrieved on 15 February 2016 from WWW.IMF.ORG/EXTERNAL/PUBS/FT/FANDD/2012/03/MORSY.HTM
5. EPI. Retrieved on 15 February 2016 from WWW.EPI.ORG/PUBLICATION/BP243/
6. U.S. Census Bureau. Retrieved on 1 July 2020 from https://www.census.gov/content/dam/Census/library/visualizations/time-series/demo/families-and-households/ad-1.pdf.

Chapter 6

1. Acuff, J. (18 September 2015). "The Office Is Dying — Good Riddance." *Time.* sourced on 1 July 2020 from https://time.com/4029874/jon-acuff-what-common-practice-will-horrify-our-kids-someday/.
2. Bureau of Labor Statistics sourced on 1 July 2020 from https://www.bls.gov/emp/education-pays-handout.pdf.
3. Information in this paragraph sourced from FRED — The Federal Reserve Economic Database, including the following:
U.S. Bureau of Labor Statistics, Unemployment Rate - Less Than a High School Diploma, 25 Yrs. & Over [LNS14027659], retrieved from FRED, Federal Reserve Bank of St. Louis; https://fred.stlouisfed.org/series/LNS14027659, June 30, 2020.
U.S. Bureau of Labor Statistics, Unemployment Rate - High School Graduates, No College, 25 Yrs. & Over [LNS14027660], retrieved from FRED, Federal Reserve Bank of St. Louis; https://fred.stlouisfed.org/series/LNS14027660, July 1, 2020.
U.S. Bureau of Labor Statistics, Unemployment Rate - Some College or Associate Degree, 25 Yrs. & Over [LNS14027689], retrieved from FRED, Federal Reserve Bank of St. Louis; https://fred.stlouisfed.org/series/LNS14027689, June 30, 2020.
U.S. Bureau of Labor Statistics, Unemployment Rate - Bachelor's Degree and Higher, 25 Yrs. & Over [LNS14027662], retrieved from FRED, Federal Reserve Bank of St. Louis; https://fred.stlouisfed.org/series/LNS14027662, July 1, 2020.
U.S. Bureau of Labor Statistics, Unemployment Rate - College Graduates - Master's Degree, 25 years and over [CGMD25O], retrieved from FRED, Federal Reserve Bank of St. Louis; https://fred.stlouisfed.org/series/CGMD25O, July 1, 2020.

ENDNOTES

Chapter 7

1. Local Area Unemployment Statistics, May 2020. Bureau Labor Statistics. Retrieved on 1 July 2020 from https://www.bls.gov/web/laus/laumstrk.htm.
2. Local Area Unemployment Statistics, May 2020. Bureau Labor Statistics. Retrieved on 1 July 2020 from https://www.bls.gov/web/metro/laummtrk.htm.
3. Source: Adobe Stock.
4. Source: Adobe Stock.

Chapter 8

1. Dahl, D. (11 Aug 2011). "Top Companies Started During a Recession." *Huffington Post*. Retrieved on 1 July 2020 from http://www.huffingtonpost.com/2010/05/10/top-companies-started-during-a-recession_n_923853.html.
2. This conceptual representation of clients and ROI was influenced by the following wonderful book: Shapiro, R. (2015). *The Power of Nice*. New York: Wiley.

Chapter 9

1. "Fast Facts and Figures About Social Security. 2017." (September 2017). Social Security Administration. Retrieved on 1 July 2020 from https://www.ssa.gov/policy/docs/chartbooks/fast_facts/2017/fast_facts17.pdf.
2. S&P Dow Jones Indices LLC, Dow Jones Industrial Average [DJIA], retrieved from FRED, Federal Reserve Bank of St. Louis; https://fred.stlouisfed.org/series/DJIA, February 15, 2016.

AUTHOR

ABOUT THE AUTHOR

Mr. Schenker is the President of Prestige Economics and Chairman of The Futurist Institute. He has been ranked one of the most accurate financial forecasters and futurists in the world. Bloomberg News has ranked Mr. Schenker a top forecaster in 43 categories, including #1 in the world for his accuracy in 25 categories, including for his forecasts of the Euro, the British Pound, the Russian Ruble, the Chinese RMB, crude oil prices, natural gas prices, gold prices, industrial metals prices, agricultural commodity prices, and U.S. jobs.

Mr. Schenker was ranked one of the top 100 most influential financial advisors in the world by Investopedia in 2018. His work has been featured in *The Wall Street Journal*, *The New York Times*, and the *Frankfurter Allgemeine Zeitung*.

He has appeared on CNBC, CNN, ABC, NBC, MSNBC, Fox, Fox Business, BNN, Bloomberg Germany, and the BBC. Mr. Schenker has been a guest host of Bloomberg Television and he is a contributor to *Bloomberg Opinion*.

Mr. Schenker attends OPEC and Fed events, and he has given keynotes for private companies, public corporations, industry groups, and the U.S. Federal Reserve. He has advised NATO and the U.S. government on the future of work, blockchain, Bitcoin, cryptocurrency, quantum computing, data analysis, forecasting, and fake news. Mr. Schenker has written 26 books. Twelve have been #1 Best Sellers, including: *The Future After COVID*, *Jobs for Robots*, *Quantum: Computing Nouveau*, *Recession-Proof*, *Electing Recession*, *Futureproof Supply Chain*, *Commodity Prices 101*, *The Future of Finance is Now*, *The Future of Energy*, *The Dumpster Fire Election*, and *The Robot and Automation Almanac* 2018 and 2020.

Mr. Schenker also wrote *The Fog of Data*, *Robot-Proof Yourself*, *Write the Future*, *Reading the Economic Tea Leaves*, and *Strategic Cost-Cutting After COVID*. Mr. Schenker was featured as one of the world's foremost futurists in the book *After Shock*.

Mr. Schenker advises executives, industry groups, institutional investors, and central banks as the President of Prestige Economics. He also founded The Futurist Institute in October 2016, for which he created a rigorous course of study that includes The Future of Work, The Future of Transportation, The Future of Data, The Future of Finance, Futurist Fundamentals, The Future of Energy, The Future of Leadership, The Future of Healthcare, The Future of Quantum Computing, The Future After COVID, and Write the Future.

Mr. Schenker is also an instructor for nine LinkedIn Learning courses on Corporate Finance, Audit and Due Diligence, Recession-Proof Career Strategies, and a weekly Economic Indicator series.

Mr. Schenker holds a Master's in Applied Economics from UNC Greensboro, a Master's in Negotiation, Conflict Resolution, and Peacebuilding from CSU Dominguez Hills, a Master's in Germanic Languages and Literature from UNC Chapel Hill, and a Bachelor's in History and German from The University of Virginia. He also holds a Certificate in FinTech from MIT, a Certificate in Supply Chain Management from MIT, a Certificate in Professional Development from UNC, a Certificate in Negotiation from Harvard Law School, a Certificate in Cybersecurity from Carnegie Mellon, and a Professional Certificate in Strategic Foresight from the University of Houston. Mr. Schenker holds the designations CMT® (Chartered Market Technician), CVA® (Certified Valuation Analyst), and CFP® (Certified Financial Planner). He is also a Certified Futurist and Long-Term Analyst™ and holds the FLTA™ designation.

Before founding Prestige Economics, Mr. Schenker worked as a Risk Specialist at McKinsey and Company, where he provided content direction to trading, risk, and commodity project teams on six continents. Prior to McKinsey, Mr. Schenker was the Chief Energy and Commodity Economist at Wachovia, which is now Wells Fargo. Based in Austin, Mr. Schenker is one of only 100 CEOs on the Texas Business Leadership Council, a non-partisan organization that advises Texas elected leadership at the state and federal level. Mr. Schenker is a Governance Fellow of the National Association of Corporate Directors. He also sits on multiple boards and is the VP of Finance on the Executive Committee of The Texas Lyceum, the preeminent non-partisan leadership group in Texas.

PRESTIGE ECONOMICS

TOP FORECASTER ACCURACY RANKINGS

Prestige Economics has been recognized as the most accurate independent commodity and financial market research firm in the world. As the only forecaster for Prestige Economics, Jason Schenker is very proud that Bloomberg News has ranked him a top forecaster in 43 different categories since 2011, including #1 in the world in 25 different forecast categories.

Mr. Schenker has been top ranked as a forecaster of economic indicators, energy prices, metals prices, agricultural prices, and foreign exchange rates.

ECONOMIC TOP RANKINGS

#1 Non-Farm Payroll Forecaster in the World
#1 New Home Sales Forecaster in the World
#2 U.S. Unemployment Rate Forecaster in the World
#3 Durable Goods Orders Forecaster in the World
#6 Consumer Confidence Forecaster in the World
#7 ISM Manufacturing Index Forecaster in the World
#7 U.S. Housing Start Forecaster in the World

ENERGY PRICE TOP RANKINGS
#1 WTI Crude Oil Price Forecaster in the World
#1 Brent Crude Oil Price Forecaster in the World
#1 Henry Hub Natural Gas Price Forecaster in the World

METALS PRICE TOP RANKINGS
#1 Gold Price Forecaster in the World
#1 Platinum Price Forecaster in the World
#1 Palladium Price Forecaster in the World
#1 Industrial Metals Price Forecaster in the World
#1 Copper Price Forecaster in the World
#1 Aluminum Price Forecaster in the World
#1 Nickel Price Forecaster in the World
#1 Tin Price Forecaster in the World
#1 Zinc Price Forecaster in the World
#2 Precious Metals Price Forecaster in the World
#2 Silver Price Forecaster in the World
#2 Lead Price Forecaster in the World
#2 Iron Ore Forecaster in the World

AGRICULTURAL PRICE TOP RANKINGS
#1 Coffee Price Forecaster in the World
#1 Cotton Price Forecaster in the World
#1 Sugar Price Forecaster in the World
#1 Soybean Price Forecaster in the World

FOREIGN EXCHANGE TOP RANKINGS

#1 Euro Forecaster in the World
#1 British Pound Forecaster in the World
#1 Swiss Franc Forecaster in the World
#1 Chinese RMB Forecaster in the World
#1 Russian Ruble Forecaster in the World
#1 Brazilian Real Forecaster in the World
#2 Turkish Lira Forecaster in the World
#3 Major Currency Forecaster in the World
#3 Canadian Dollar Forecaster in the World
#4 Japanese Yen Forecaster in the World
#5 Australian Dollar Forecaster in the World
#7 Mexican Peso Forecaster in the World
#1 EURCHF Forecaster in the World
#2 EURJPY Forecaster in the World
#2 EURGBP Forecaster in the World
#2 EURRUB Forecaster in the World

More information about Prestige Economics:
www.prestigeeconomics.com

THE FUTURIST INSTITUTE

 THE FUTURIST INSTITUTE

The Futurist Institute was founded in 2016 to help analysts, executives, and professionals incorporate technology and trend risks and opportunities into their strategic planning. The Futurist Institute confers the Futurist and Long-Term Analyst™ (FLTA) designation and helps analysts become Certified Futurists™. Our courses have been approved for continuing education hours by the Certified Financial Planner Board of Standards (CFP Board), Global Association of Risk Professionals (GARP), and National Association of Certified Valuators and Analysts (NACVA).

Current Courses

The Future After COVID
The Future of Work
The Future of Data
The Future of Energy
The Future of Finance
The Future of Healthcare
The Future of Leadership
The Future of Transportation
Futurist Fundamentals
Quantum Computing
Write the Future

Visit The Futurist Institute
www.futuristinstitute.org

PUBLISHER

Prestige Professional Publishing was founded in 2011 to produce insightful and timely professional reference books. We are registered with the Library of Congress.

Published Titles

Be the Shredder, Not the Shred
Commodity Prices 101
Electing Recession
Financial Risk Management Fundamentals
Futureproof Supply Chain
A Gentle Introduction to Audit and Due Diligence
Jobs for Robots
Midterm Economics
Quantum: Computing Nouveau
Reading the Economic Tea Leaves
Recession-Proof Career Strategies After COVID
Robot-Proof Yourself
Spikes: Growth Hacking Leadership
Strategic Cost-Cutting
Strategic Cost-Cutting After COVID
The Dumpster Fire Election
The Fog of Data
The Future After COVID
The Future of Energy
The Future of Finance is Now
The Promise of Blockchain
Write the Future

PUBLISHER

Published Titles

The Robot and Automation Almanac — 2018
The Robot and Automation Almanac — 2019
The Robot and Automation Almanac — 2020

Forthcoming Titles

Content Monster
Disruption Warfare
The Brain Business
The Economics of Revolt and Revolution
The Future of Agriculture
The Future of Healthcare
The Future of Travel and Leisure

THE FUTURE AFTER COVID

The Future After COVID provides strategic perspectives on the impact of COVID-19 on numerous industries, the economy, and business. *The Future After COVID* was published in April 2020. This book has been a #1 New Release on Amazon, and it has been featured on Bloomberg Radio.

READING THE ECONOMIC TEA LEAVES

In *Reading the Economic Tea Leaves,* Jason Schenker helps readers understand economic indicators and what economic data and reports imply about for industries, financial markets, policy, and jobs. This book was published by Prestige Professional Publishing in August 2019.

JOBS FOR ROBOTS

Jobs for Robots provides an in-depth look at the future of automation and robots, with a focus on the opportunities as well as the risks ahead. Job creation in coming years will be extremely strong for the kind of workers that do not require payroll taxes, healthcare, or vacation: robots. *Jobs for Robots* was published in February 2017. This book has been a #1 Bestseller on Amazon.

DISCLAIMER

FROM THE AUTHOR

The following disclaimer applies to any content in this book:

This book is commentary intended for general information use only and is not investment advice. Jason Schenker does not make recommendations on any specific or general investments, investment types, asset classes, non-regulated markets, specific equities, bonds, or other investment vehicles. Jason Schenker does not guarantee the completeness or accuracy of analyses and statements in this book, nor does Jason Schenker assume any liability for any losses that may result from the reliance by any person or entity on this information. Opinions, forecasts, and information are subject to change without notice. This book does not represent a solicitation or offer of financial or advisory services or products; this book is only market commentary intended and written for general information use only. This book does not constitute investment advice. All links were correct and active at the time this book was published.

DISCLAIMER

FROM THE PUBLISHER

The following disclaimer applies to any content in this book:

This book is commentary intended for general information use only and is not investment advice. Prestige Professional Publishing, LLC does not make recommendations on any specific or general investments, investment types, asset classes, non-regulated markets, specific equities, bonds, or other investment vehicles. Prestige Professional Publishing, LLC does not guarantee the completeness or accuracy of analyses and statements in this book, nor does Prestige Professional Publishing, LLC assume any liability for any losses that may result from the reliance by any person or entity on this information. Opinions, forecasts, and information are subject to change without notice. This book does not represent a solicitation or offer of financial or advisory services or products; this book is only market commentary intended and written for general information use only. This book does not constitute investment advice. All links were correct and active at the time this book was published.

Prestige Professional Publishing, LLC

4412 City Park Road #4

Austin, Texas 78730

www.prestigeprofessionalpublishing.com

ISBN: 978-1-946197-60-3 *Paperback*
   978-1-946197-57-3 *Ebook*